Best Wishes,
Robert Wilson

WALL!

# The Best Graffiti Off The Walls Of America

Collected by Ken Frankel & Robert Wilson
Designed and Illustrated by Bob Salo

Longstreet Press • Atlanta

Published by
LONGSTREET PRESS, INC.
A subsidiary of Cox Newspapers,
A division of Cox Enterprises, Inc.
2140 Newmarket Parkway
Suite 118
Marietta, GA 30067



Library of Congress Catalog Card Number: 96-76033



ISBN: 1-56352-323-X

First printing 1996

Book and jacket design by Bob Salo

Printed in the United States of America

Digital film prep and separations by Advertising Technologies, Inc., Atlanta, GA

This book is dedicated
to everyone who maintains
the fine tradition of writing
witticisms on bathroom walls.

## Acknowledgements

This book was made possible, in part, by the help of these friends
who shared with us the graffiti they discovered on the walls of America:

**Debra Dixon**
**John Dwyer**
**John Fant**
**Peter C. Johnson**
**George Johnson**
**Karen Johnson**
**Robert Kahn**
**Donny Lea**
**Tony Lea**
**Pat Raffalovitch**
**William D. Shaw**
**Martin Stone**
**Kris Sypher**
**Brian Vonn**
**Jim Wilson**

Special thanks to **Martin Stone** whose photography helped us capture
the special images we wanted to emulate in this book;
to **John Kirkland** for assisting us with props;
and to **Steve Maddern** for art critique and encouragement.

# contents

**The graffiti reproduced in this book was collected over the past 20 years in our travels around the United States.** Most we found, but others were given to us by friends. Some we copied onto the backs of matchbook covers, business cards and cocktail napkins; others we simply memorized. Many of the places where we discovered them are now out of business; some we've merely forgotten and some came from such boring places that we've attempted to amuse the reader with fictious locations.

Often the witticisms we found turned out to be famous, so where appropriate and when possible, we have made every effort to determine the original authorship. Any famous quotation or copyrighted material that we have not credited is unintentional and we extend our apologies to the authors. To those people, and their families, please accept that your words were of such value to the person who penned them (albeit on a bathroom wall) that he or she wanted to share them with others.

# fore word

*Contrary to popular belief, I'm not the one who originated the idea of writing on walls.*

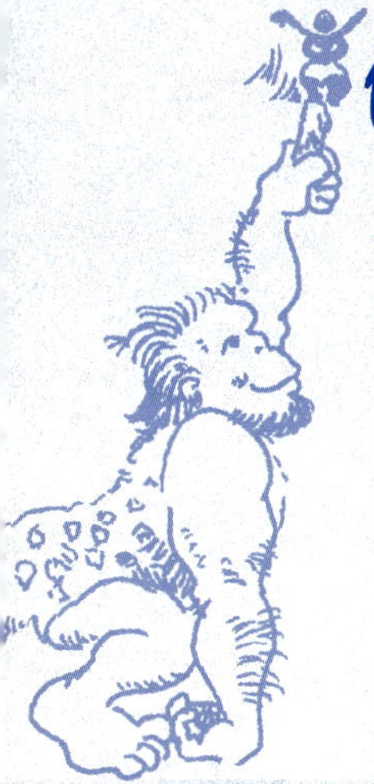

Oh, maybe I popularized it back during the Big One (that's WWII for you generation Xer's), but graffiti is as old as written language (and perhaps older). It's been found on the walls of Pompeii, in the ruins of ancient Egypt, Rome and Greece, and don't forget that caveman graffiti in France. In fact, the word graffiti comes from the Greek word for "scratch" because back then they didn't have pens or spray paint, so they scratched their prose into stone walls.

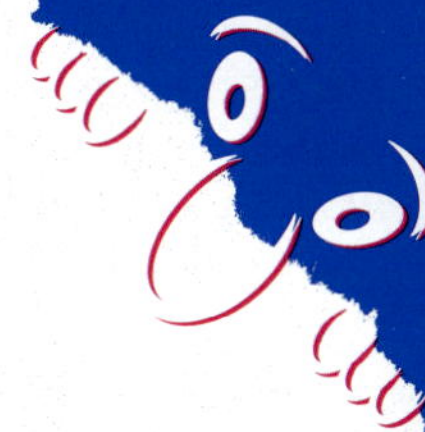

**BY KILROY . . .**

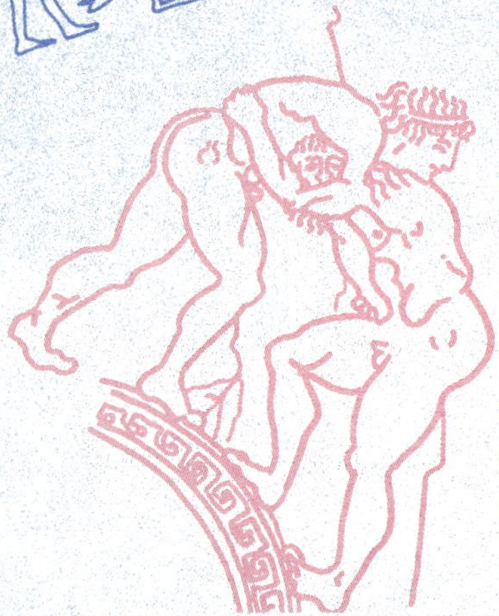

Archaeologists get particularly excited when they find graffiti. They consider it a highly valuable find because graffiti reveals the vernacular of an era... unedited thoughts written from the heart (or lower). As an enduring artifact, graffiti gives us a clearer picture of a people than the usual sanitized documents and revised accounts.

You may wonder why people write on walls (and in our case lavatory walls). Could it be that the inherent privacy of a restroom stall encourages cogitation on man's condition, or is all that space merely another thing we're attempting to fill?

Some write to vent their rage, and others to rehearse their wit. But sometimes the solitude of a stall becomes the sounding board for new ideas gathering critical mass. It could be called the last great medium for pure self-expression, and perhaps the only way for anonymous authors to hold a captive audience.

So, if graffiti is art and art reflects life, then what are we seeing in this odd mirror? Some may say that graffiti reflects the coarser levels of our culture, but as you read on, decide for yourself what social commentary these scrawls make about our civilization.

We hope this collection will satisfy the curiosity of women who wonder what really happens in the sanctity of a men's room stall, and we hope it will serve as a reminder for men who have forgotten what writing on walls is all about. And let's face it, ultimately, this book is for anyone looking for a good chuckle.

Like many other fine books, **Off The Wall** is meant to be put on display, to be placed in a cherished spot where friends and neighbors can admire its beauty and absorb its wisdom. So don't put it on your coffee table; put it where it truly belongs: in the bathroom!

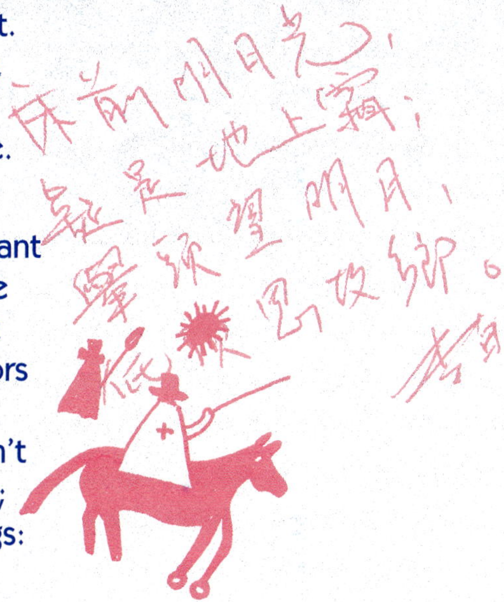


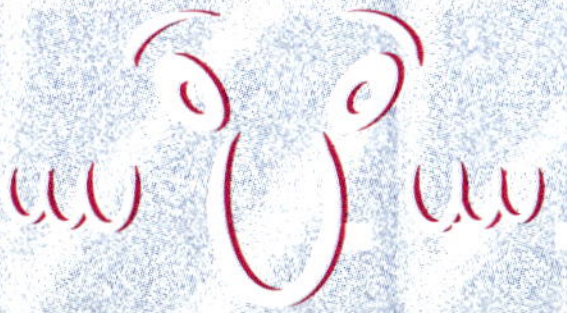

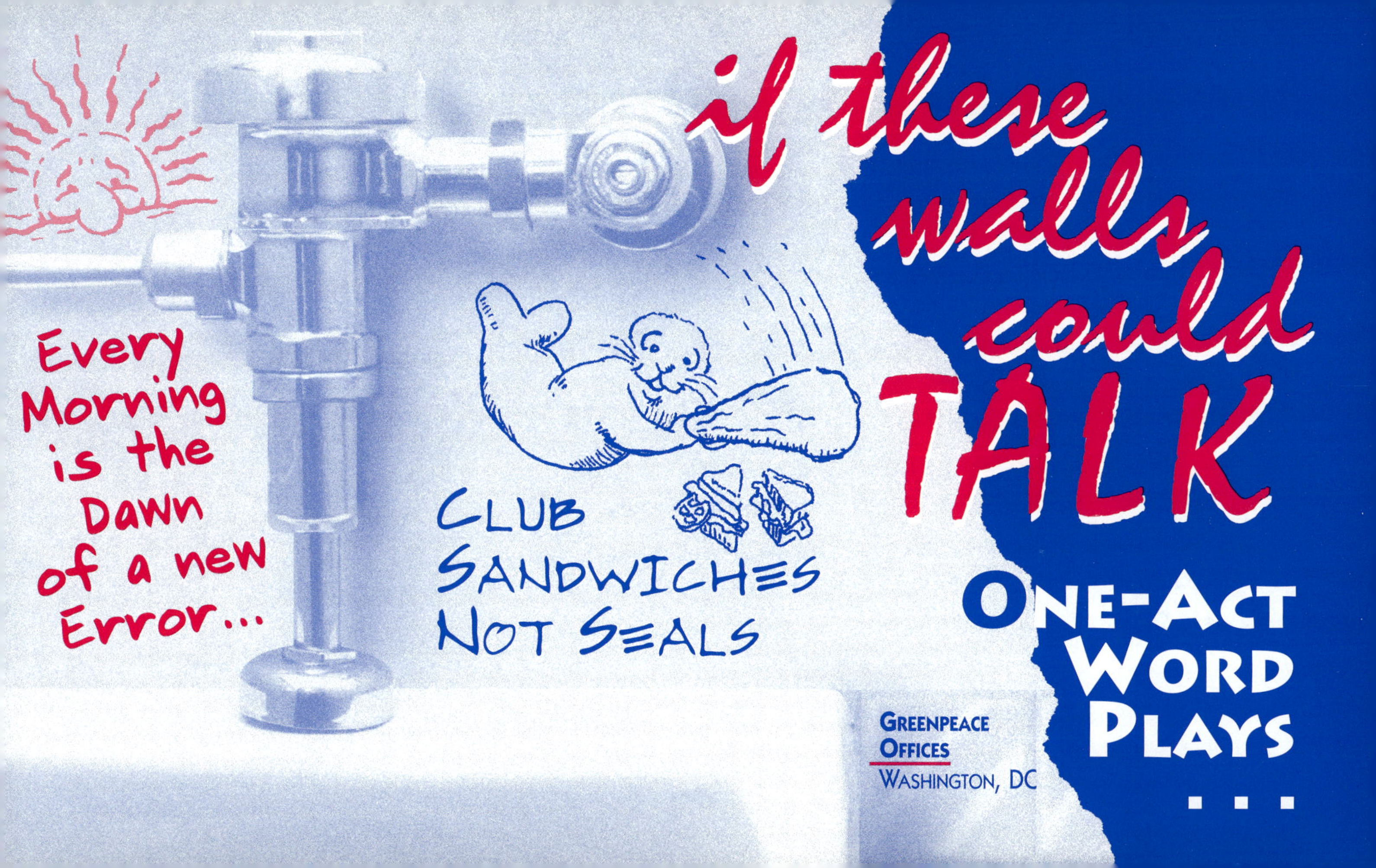
if these walls could TALK
ONE-ACT WORD PLAYS . . .
Every Morning is the Dawn of a new Error...
CLUB SANDWICHES NOT SEALS
GREENPEACE OFFICES
WASHINGTON, DC

Sticks and stones may break my bones--

but names involve my LAWYER.

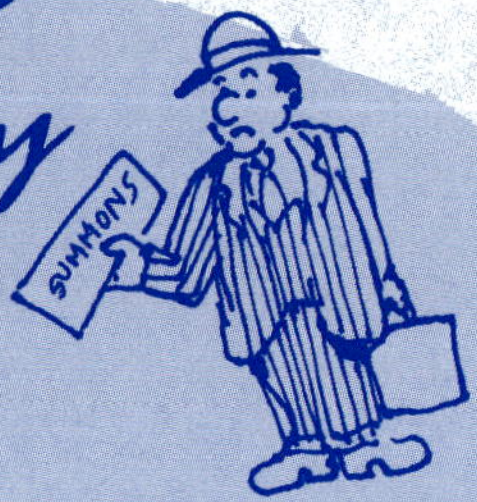


**ALTERNATIVELY:**

"STICKS AND STONES MAY BREAK MY BONES, BUT NAMES WILL GET YOU SUED FOR LIBEL." DOESN'T RHYME, IS MUCH LESS FUN, AND SOUNDS LIKE A LAWYER WROTE IT.

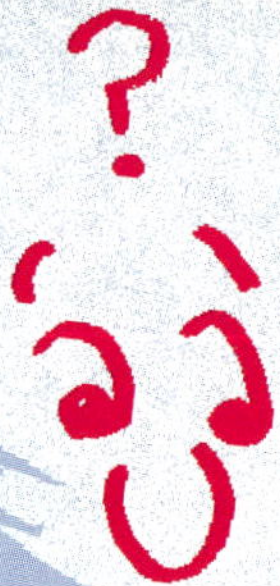

VU JA DE:

The strange feeling that you've never been here before.

Mental floss prevents Moral Decay.

**L.A. COUNTY COURTHOUSE**
LOS ANGELES, CALIFORNIA

**HIGHWAY 190 REST STOP**
NEAR EL DORADO, TEXAS

**HERITAGE USA**
NORTH CAROLINA

Proofread carefully to see if you any words out.

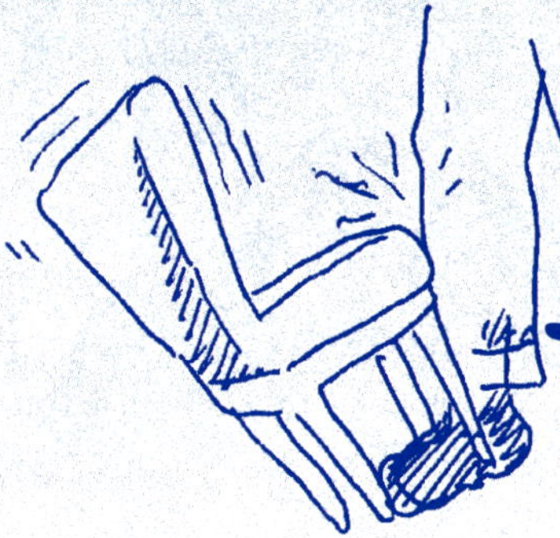

SHIN: a device for finding furniture in the dark

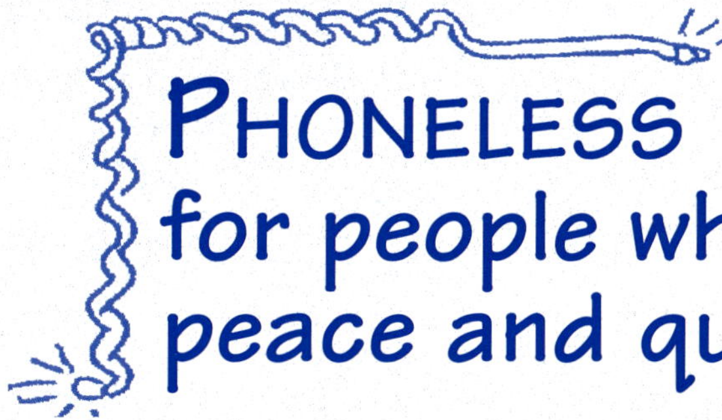

PHONELESS CORD: for people who like peace and quiet.

**TIME-WARNER HEADQUARTERS**
NEW YORK , NEW YORK

**AT&T BELL LABS**
NEW YORK, NEW YORK

**FURNITURE SHOWROOM REST ROOM**
HIGH POINT, NORTH CAROLINA

999

Mark of the Dyslexic Beast.

Dysletics Untie!

DAM: Mothers Against Dyslexia

I've been up all night contemplating the existence of DOG.

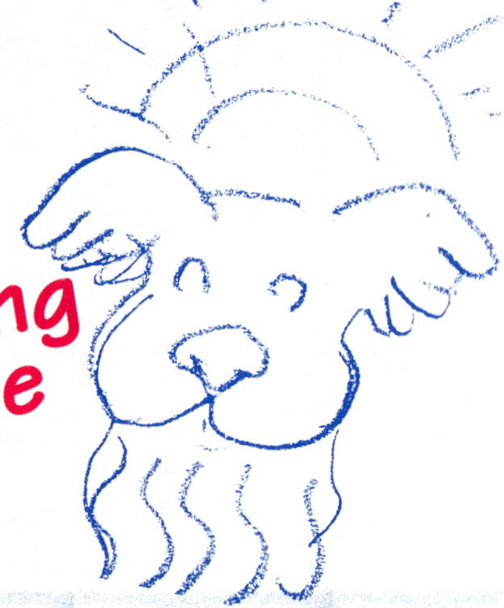

Dept. of Speech Pathology
Tufts University
Medford, Massachusetts

Why is "abbreviation" such a long word?

Men's lavatory
U.S. Capitol
Washington, D.C.

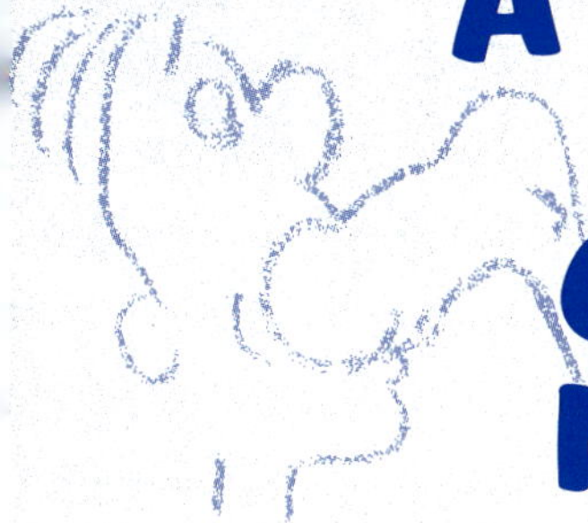

**A Closed Mouth Gathers No Feet**

VARIETY
COVER STORY

CHRISTOPHER ROBIN TAKES OVER DISNEY STUDIOS IN POOH D'ETAT.

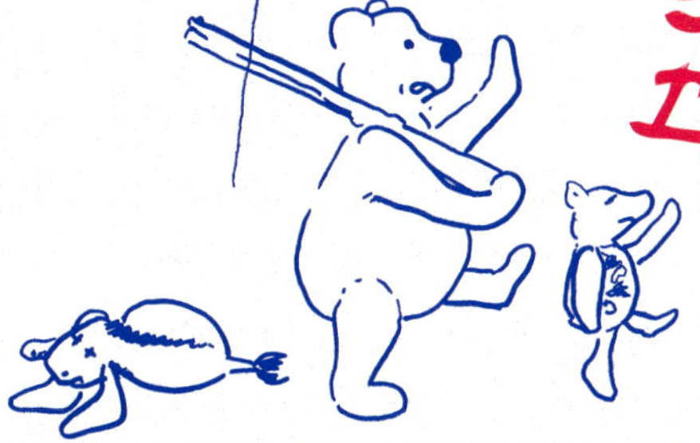

Universal Studios
Orlando, Florida

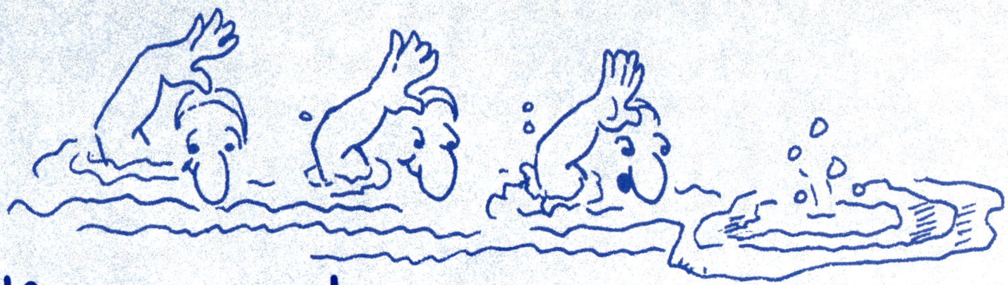

If one synchronized swimmer drowns, do the rest have to drown too?

The Age Old Question of Sync or Swim.

Nostalgia isn't what it used to be.

I WISH I WERE WHAT I WAS WHEN I WAS TRYING TO BECOME WHAT I AM NOW.

The deaf man heard the dumb man say that

**OLYMPIC NATATORIUM**
ATLANTA, GEORGIA

**DAR HEADQUARTERS**
PHILADELPHIA , PENNSYLVANIA

Don't use a big word when a diminutive one will suffice.

You can pick your friends...
You can pick your nose...
But you cannot pick
your friend's nose.

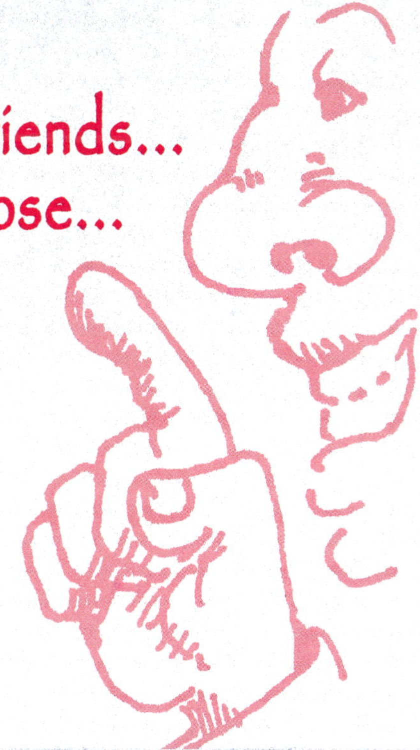

Don't use no double negatives.

the blind man saw the lame man run.

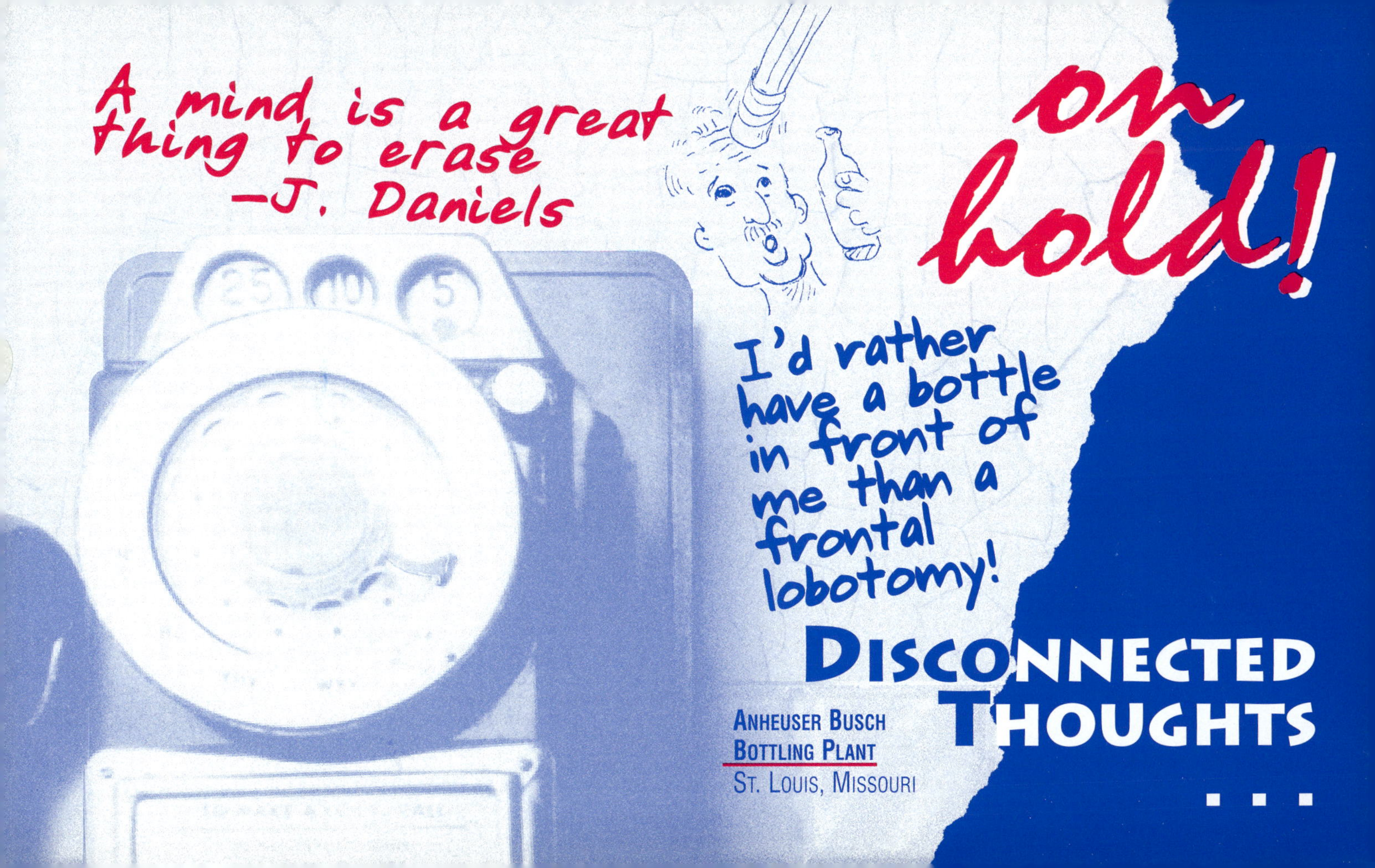
A mind is a great thing to erase
—J. Daniels
on hold!
I'd rather have a bottle in front of me than a frontal lobotomy!
DISCONNECTED THOUGHTS
...
ANHEUSER BUSCH
BOTTLING PLANT
ST. LOUIS, MISSOURI

I can see clearly now, the brain is gone...

I have high friends in places.

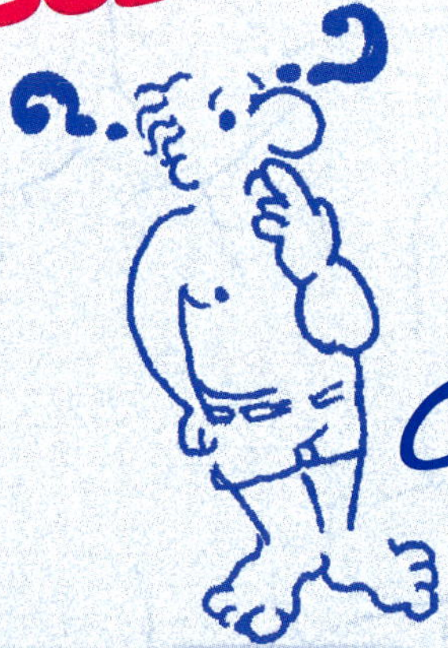

24 hours in a day... 24 beers in a case... COINCIDENCE?

**Harley's Hog Bar**
Oakland, California

**Men's Lounge City Hall**
New York, New York

**QuickMart**
Dallas, Texas

REALITY is for people who can't handle DRUGS.

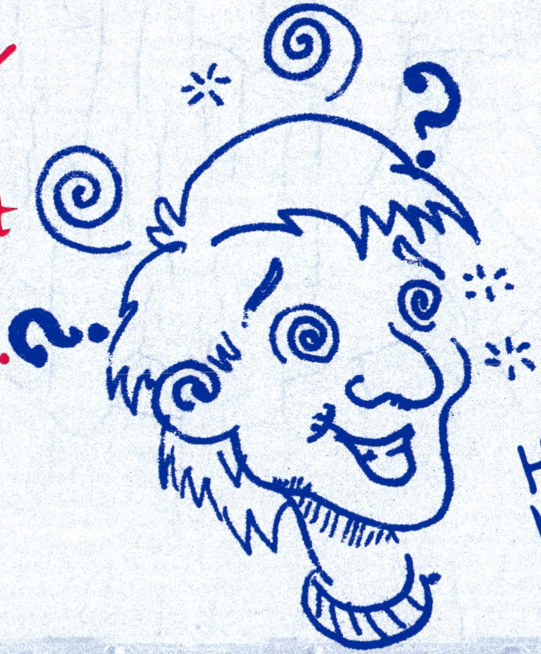

GETTING DRUNK IS THE ANSWER... I FORGET THE QUESTION.

He who hesitates... is stoned.

**ESALEN INSTITUTE**
PALO ALTO, CALIFORNIA

**CAFE EREWHON**
ATLANTA, GEORGIA

I'd explain it to you, but your brain would EXPLODE.

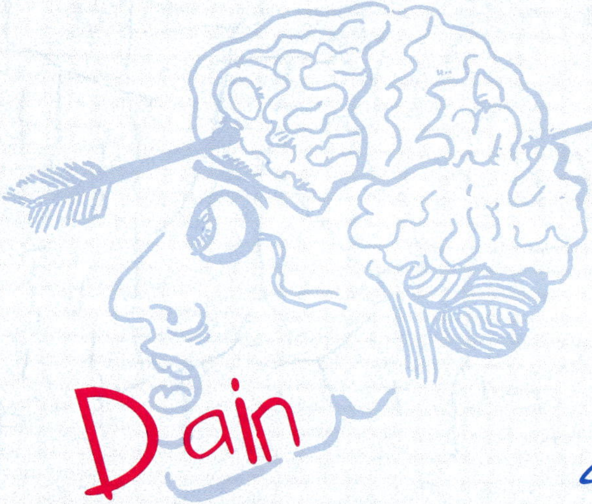

Dain Bramaged.

Ever stop to think... and forget to start again!?

**Philosophy Department, Dartmouth College**
Hanover, New Hampshire

**Psychology Lab, Cornell University**
Ithaca, New York

**Brookings Institution**
Washington, D.C.

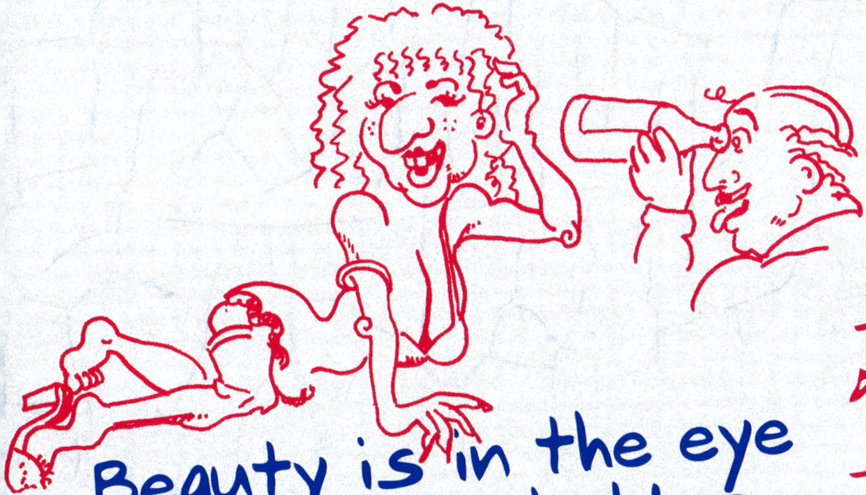

Beauty is in the eye of the beer holder.

I feel more like I did when I got here than I do now.

I'm not as think as you stoned I am...

**The Meet Market**
Miami, Florida

**Bus Station**
Charlottesville, Virginia

**The Colliseum**
After a Grateful Dead concert.

# TOP 10 REASONS WHY BEER IS BETTER THAN WOMEN:

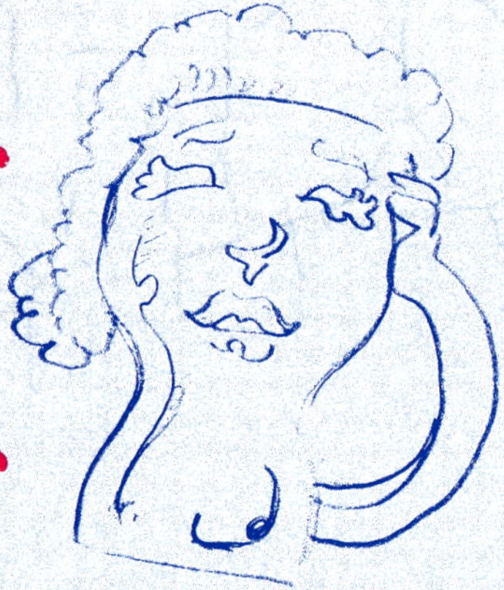

10. You can always pick up a beer in a bar.
9. A frigid beer is a good beer.
8. Beer can't give you the clap.
7. Beer doesn't get headaches.

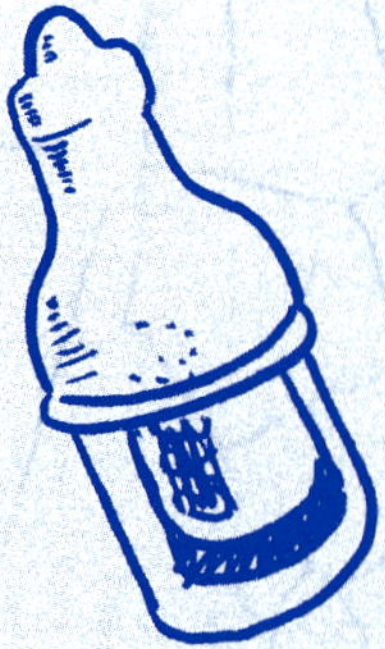

6. Beer is good any "time of the month."

5. You don't have to marry a beer.

4. You don't have to feel guilty about having more than one beer a night.

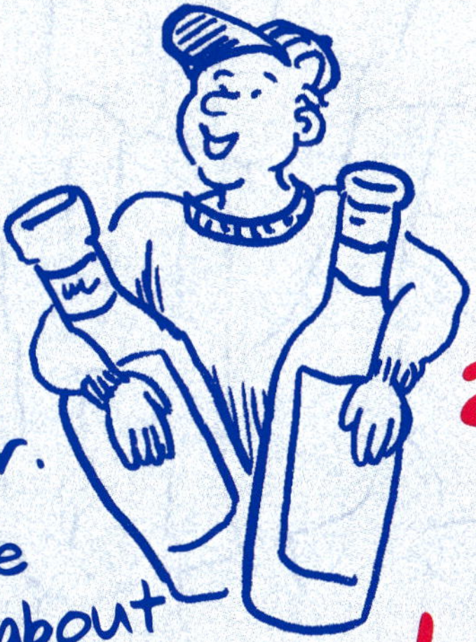

3. A beer doesn't get jealous when you grab another beer.

2. If you switch beers, you don't have to pay alimony.

1. A beer will always let you take its top off.

COMPILED FROM VARIOUS BARS AROUND THE COUNTRY

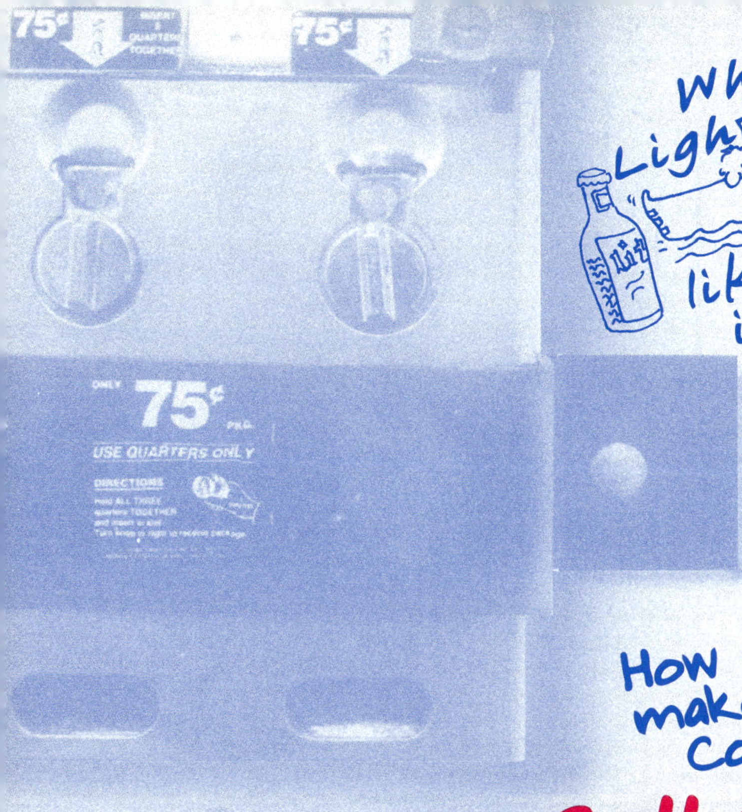


# below the borscht belt

Why is Light Beer

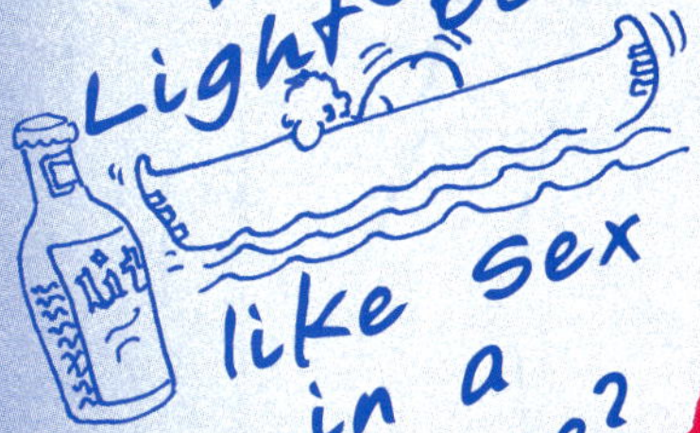

like sex in a canoe?

Both are F—king close to water!

How do you make a cop come?

Call 911!

CASTRO STREET POLICE PRECINCT
SAN FRANCISCO, CALIFORNIA

## THESE USED TO BE A DIME A DOZEN . . .

How do you Get a Nun PREGNANT?

Dress her like an ALTAR BOY!

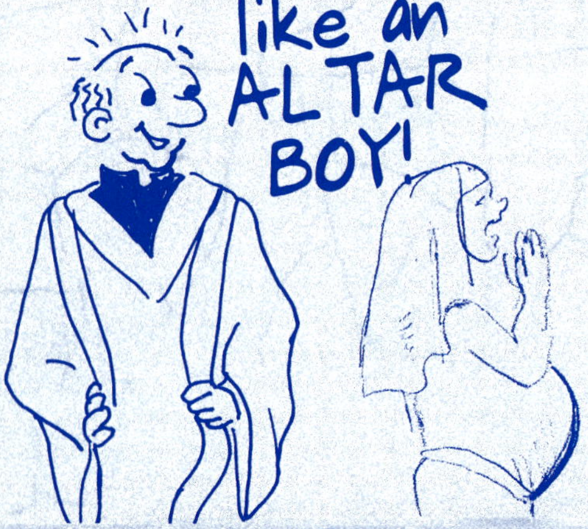

what's the difference between a pigeon and a farmer?

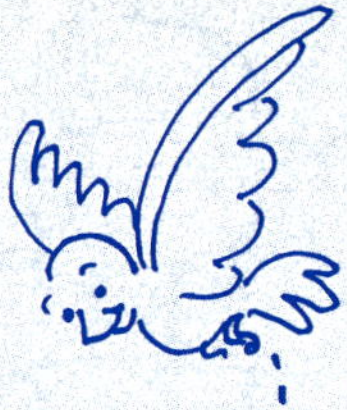

A pigeon can make a small deposit on a tractor!

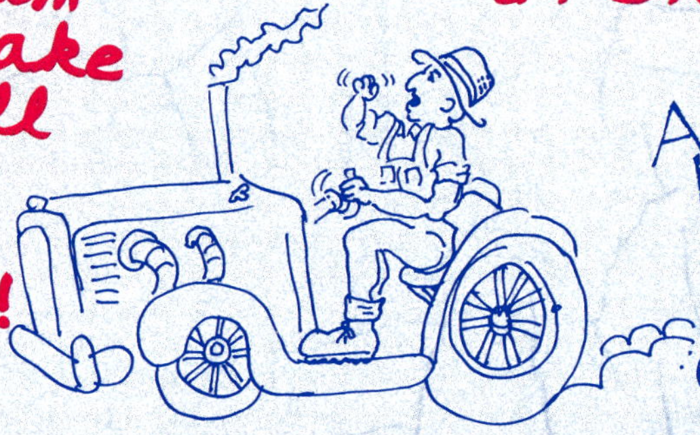

What's the difference between a BMW and a PORCUPINE?

A porcupine has pricks on the OUTSIDE!

**St. Phillips Episcopal Rectory**
Providence, Rhode Island

**4-H Clubhouse**
Enid, Oklahoma

WHAT'S THE DIFFERENCE BETWEEN A WAITRESS AND A PROCTOLOGIST?

A PROCTOLOGIST ONLY HAS TO WORK WITH ONE ASSHOLE AT A TIME.

**EMPLOYEE'S RESTROOM**
**WAFFLE HOUSE ON I-85**

NEAR ANDERSON,
SOUTH CAROLINA

HOW MANY BIRDS CAN YOU GET UNDER A SCOTSMAN'S KILT?

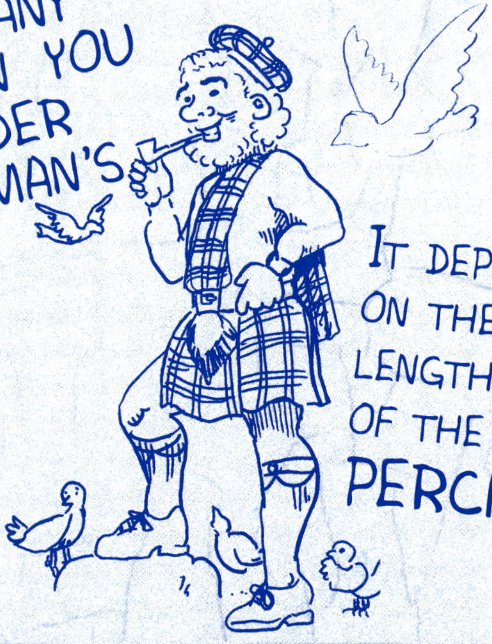

IT DEPENDS ON THE LENGTH OF THE PERCH!

**PORT-O-LET AT**
**HIGHLAND GAMES**
**SCOTTISH FESTIVAL**

STONE MOUNTAIN,
GEORGIA

Why shouldn't blind people sky dive?

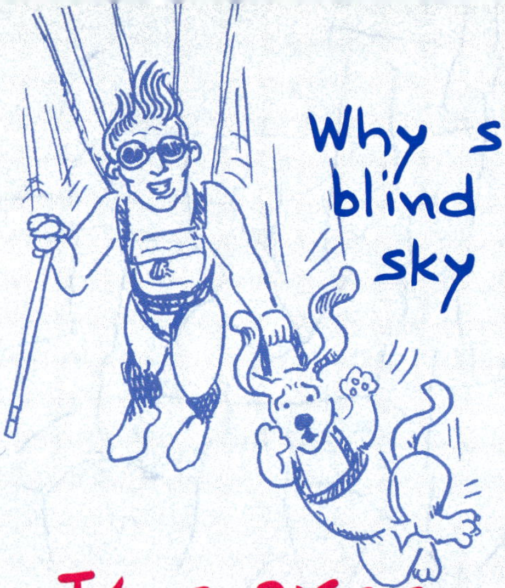

It scares the crap out of their dogs.

NORTHWINDS SKYDIVING ACADEMY
CHICAGO, ILLINOIS

WHY DO DOGS LICK THEMSELVES?

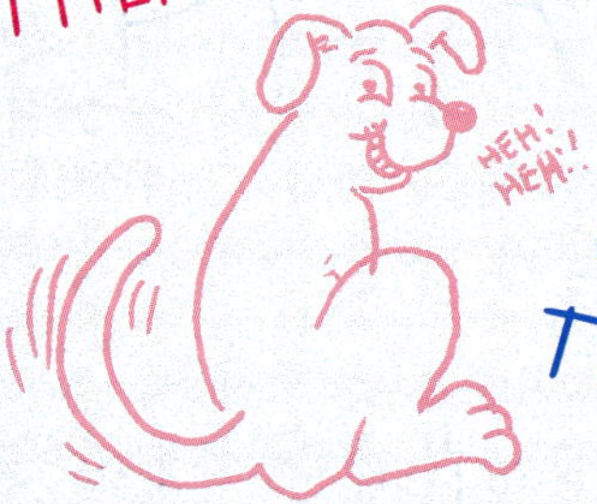


BECAUSE THEY CAN.

What is the difference between a poodle and a pitbull humping your leg?

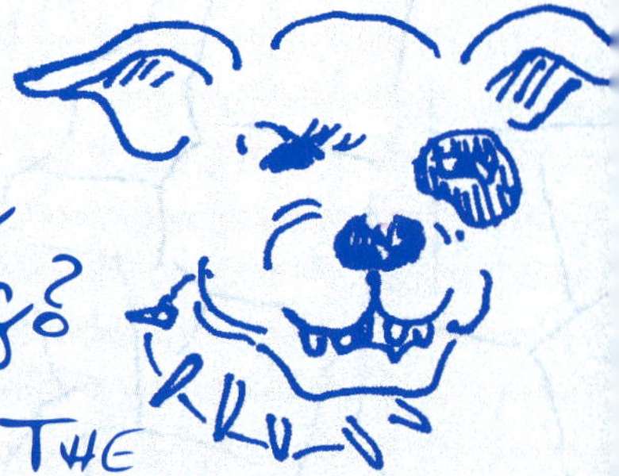

THE PITBULL GETS TO FINISH!

AMERICAN KENNEL CLUB 100TH ANNUAL DOG SHOW
LAS VEGAS, NEVADA

WHAT IS THE BEST METHOD OF BIRTH CONTROL?

Use your HEAD.

**STAIRWELL AT PLANNED PARENTHOOD OFFICE**
TULSA, OKLAHOMA

what would Elvis be doing right now if he were alive?

Scratching like HELL on the lid of his coffin.

**GULF STATION MEN'S ROOM**
MEMPHIS, TENNESSEE

WHY IS THE USS ENTERPRISE LIKE TOILET PAPER?

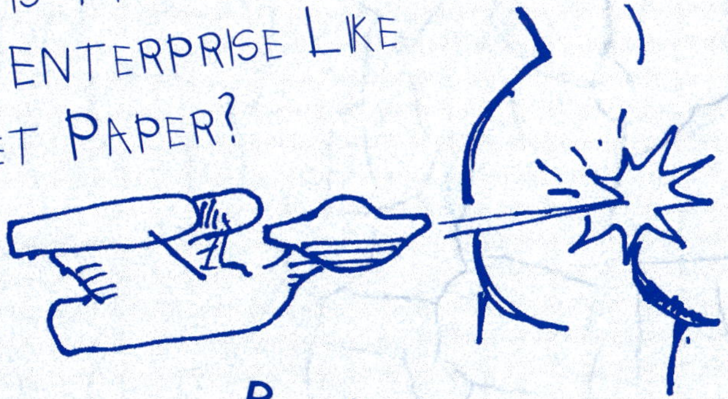

Both wipe out KLNGONS around URANUS.

**FRESHMAN DORM, COLGATE UNIVERSITY**
HAMILTON, NEW YORK

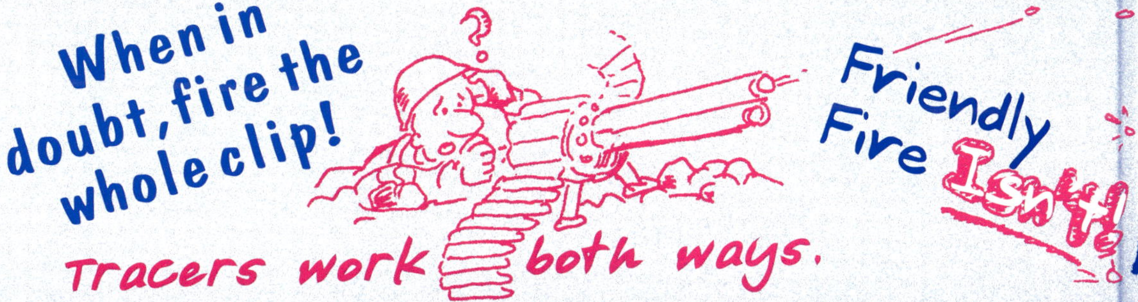


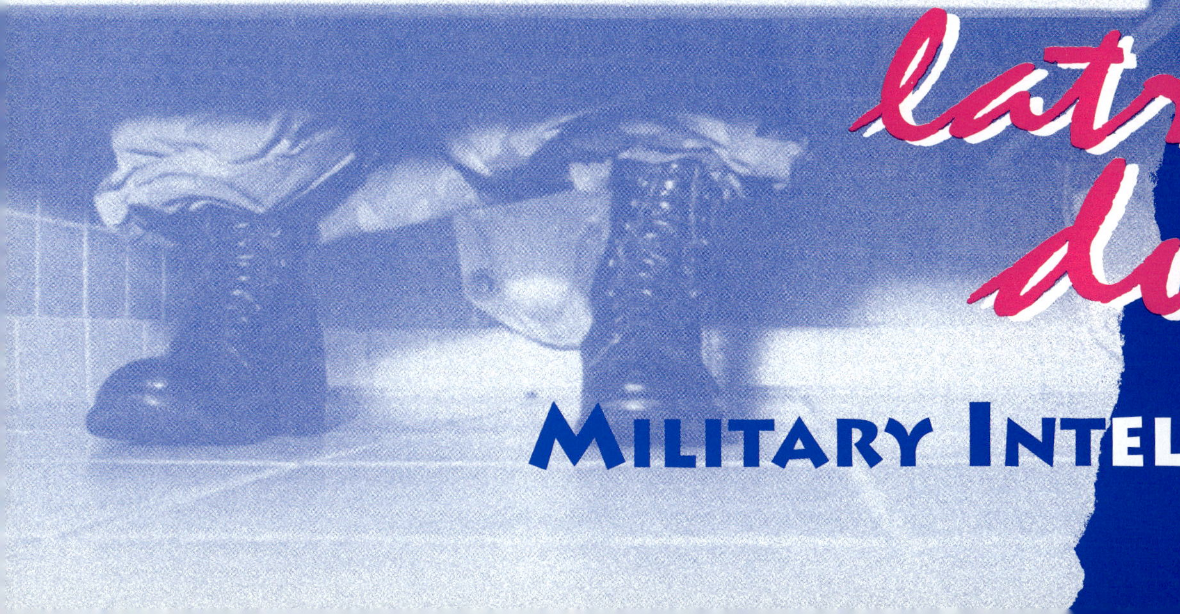

# latrine duty

## MILITARY INTELLIGENCE

. . .

## M.A.R.I.N.E.

Muscles Are Required
Intelligence Not Essential

**Marine HQ**
Quantico, Virginia

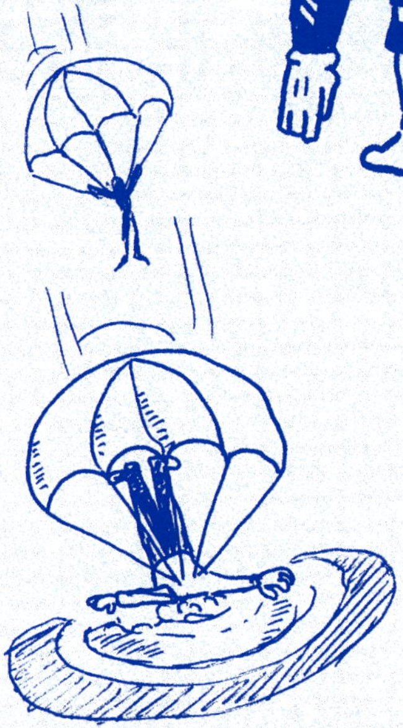

## Airborne = Lawn Darts

**Fort Bragg**
North Carolina

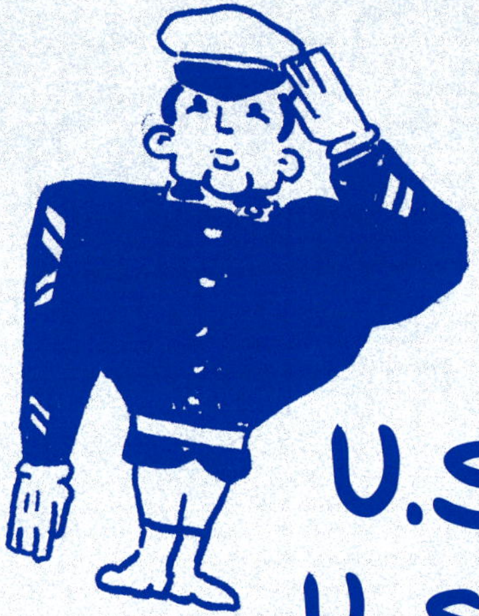

## U.S.M.C.

U Signed the MF-ing Contract

**Marine Boot Camp Barracks**
Parris Island, South Carolina

Artillery = a five-mile sniper

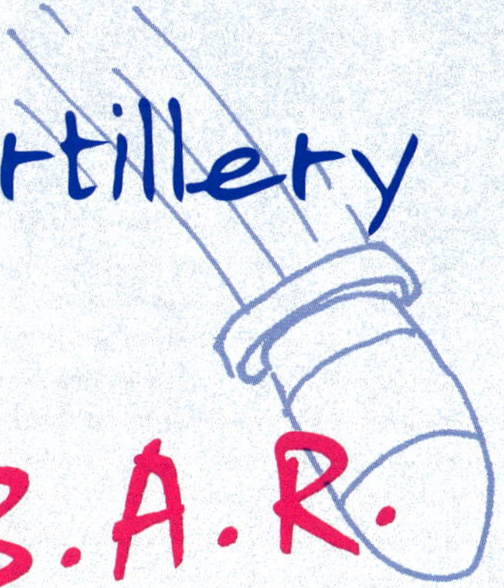

F.U.B.A.R.

Fouled Up Beyond All Recognition

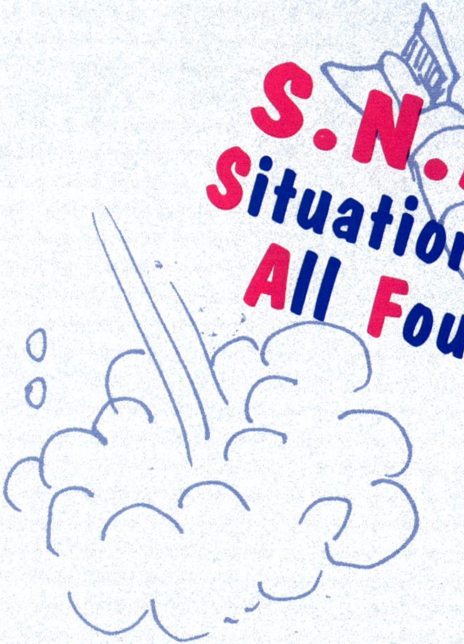

S.N.A.F.U.

Situation Normal-All Fouled Up

**Offutt AFB**
Omaha, Nebraska

*Incoming missiles have the right of way!*

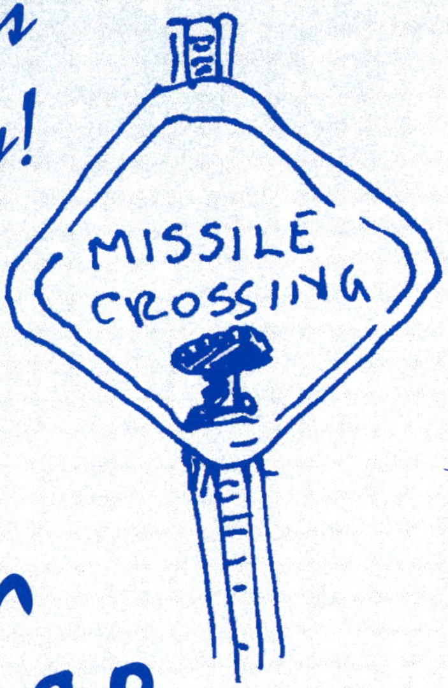


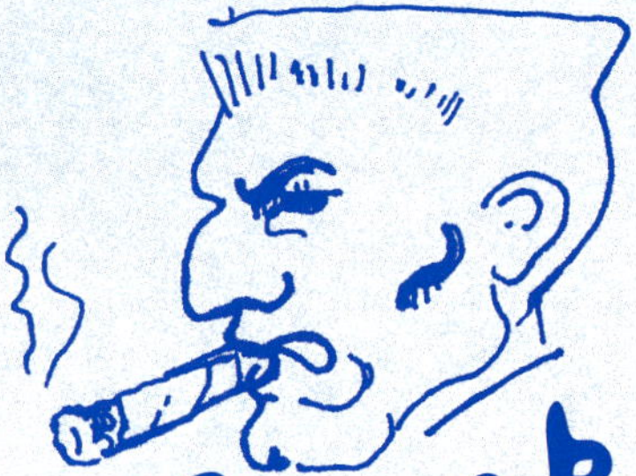

Smoke 'em like a cheap cigar.

**Nose of F-15 Eagle, Robbins Air Force Base**
Georgia

# BEER MATH

One platoon
× 3 beers
= 37 cases

(For you civilians, a platoon is about 23 guys)

**PX, Ft. Benning**
Georgia

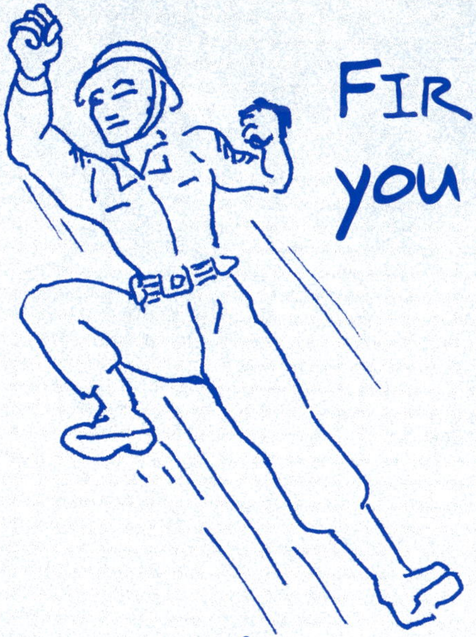

First Rule of Combat: you are **NOT** Superman.

Field experience is something you don't get until just after you need it.

No combat ready group has <u>ever</u> passed inspection.

**Barracks**
**Guantanamo Naval Base**
Guantanamo Bay, Cuba

# Murphy's Laws of Combat:

Murphy was a grunt!

...Anything you do can get you shot... including **nothing.**

...If your attack is going well... you've walked into an **ambush.**

...No matter which way you have to march... it's always **uphill.**

...The easy way is always mined.

**NAVAL AIR STATION**
JACKSONVILLE, FLORIDA

...The worse the weather... the more likely you'll have to be in it.

**ENLISTED MEN'S BAR, FORT STEWART**
GEORGIA

# There is no such thing as an atheist in a foxhole.

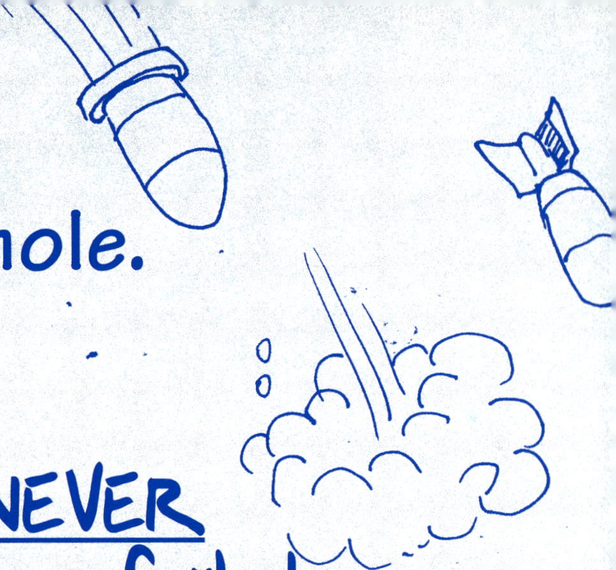

*Make it tough for the enemy to get in ... and you won't be able to get out.*

FT. DIX
NEW JERSEY

**NEVER**
share a foxhole
with anyone
BRAVER
than YOURSELF.

Tank drivers call infantry men TRACK GREASE

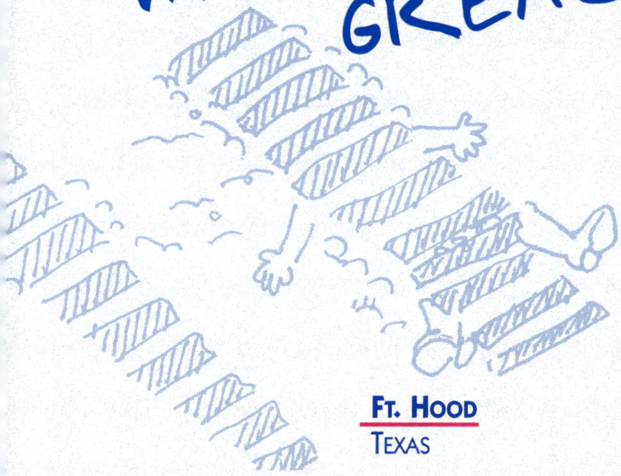

**FT. HOOD**
TEXAS

Never draw fire — it irritates everyone around you.

Don't forget: Your weapon was made by the lowest bidder.

**MEN'S ROOM, THE PENTAGON**
WASHINGTON, D.C.

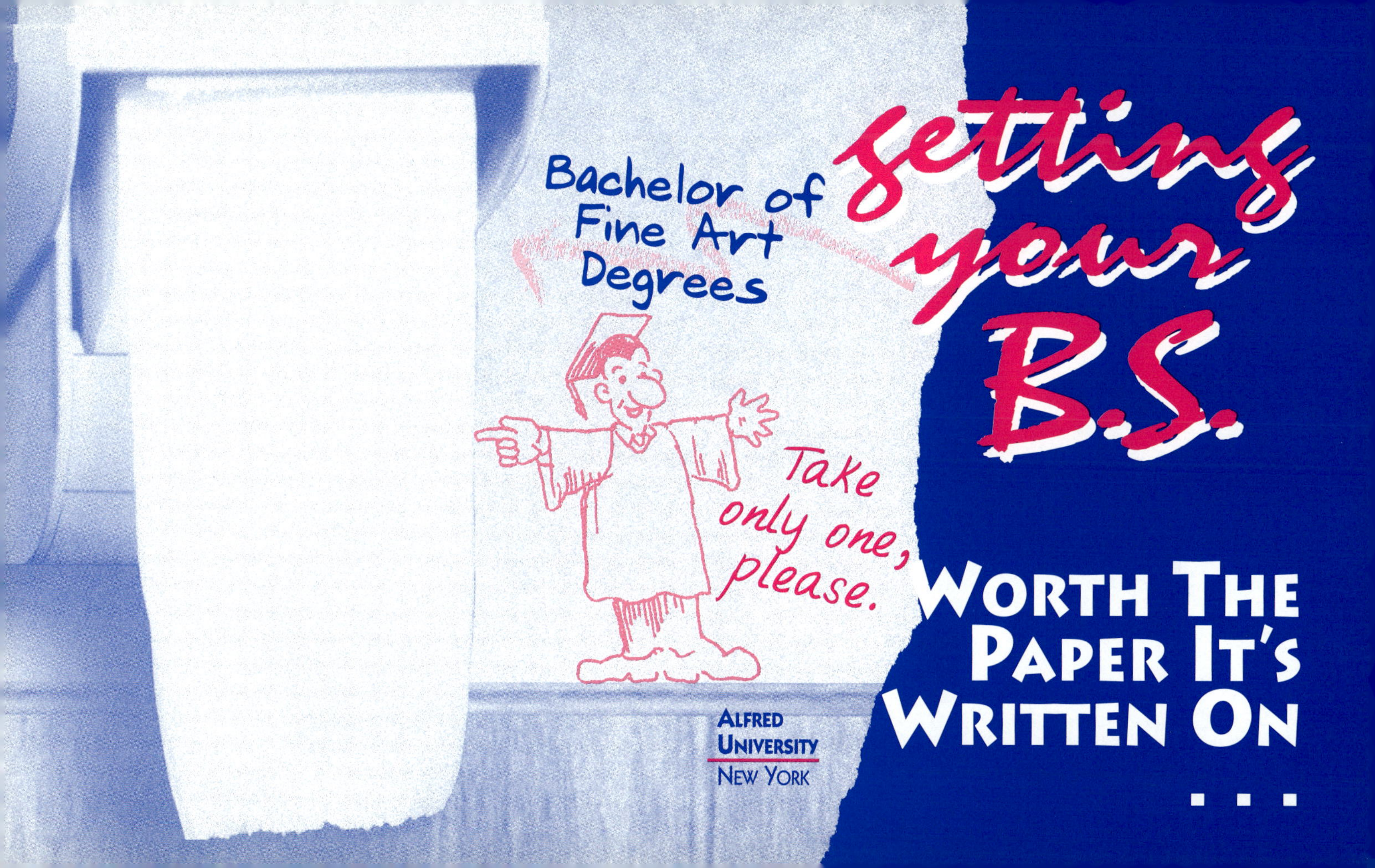

Bachelor of Fine Art Degrees
getting your B.S.
Take only one, please.
WORTH THE PAPER IT'S WRITTEN ON . . .
ALFRED UNIVERSITY NEW YORK

Why do UGA grads put their diplomas in the windows of their cars?

So they can park in handicap spaces.

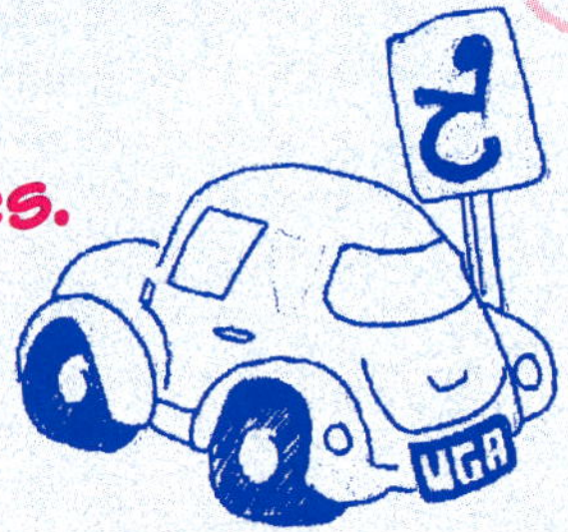


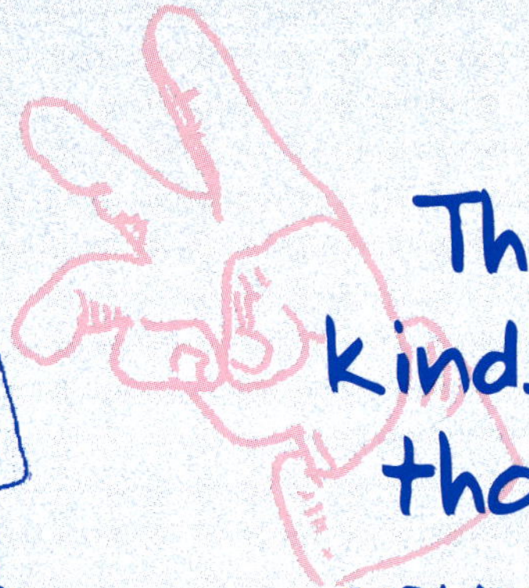

There are 3 kinds of people: those who can count and those who can't.

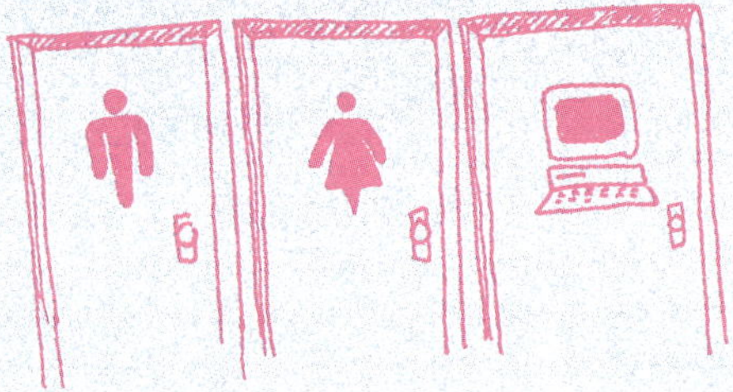

Will the Information Super Highway have any rest stops?

**Georgia Institute of Technology**
Atlanta, Georgia

**Locker Room, Michigan State University Athletic Center**
East Lansing, Michigan

Physics Test Question:

Define the Universe and give three examples.

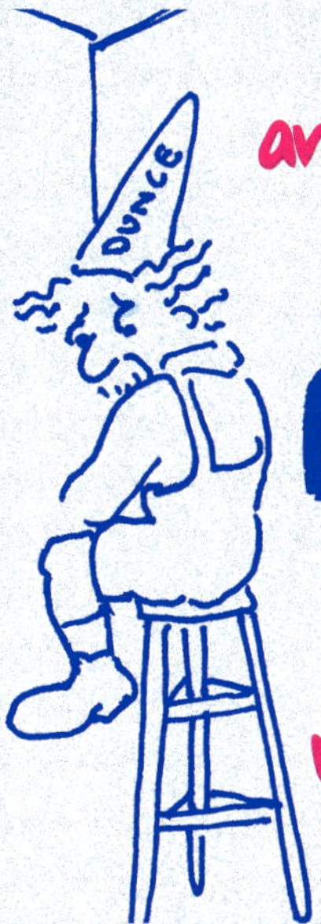


$E = MC^2$

F

Next time, Albert, show your work!

If you're not part of the solution—

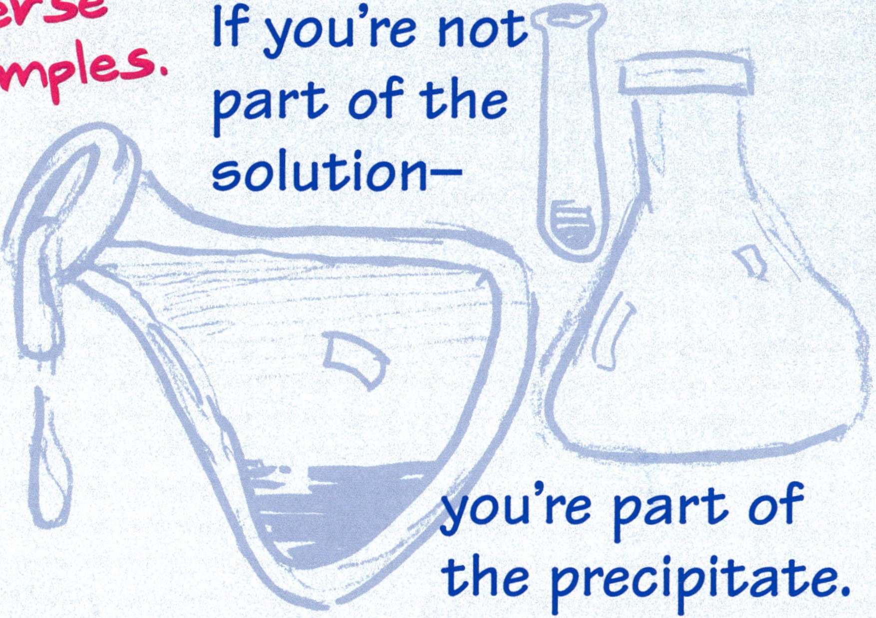

you're part of the precipitate.

**Chemistry Lab at Cal Tech**
Pasadena, California

Gravity is not an option - It's the LAW.

**Kennedy Space Center**
Cape Canaveral, Florida

Don't blame me for gravity. I voted for velcro!

There is no gravity - the earth sucks.

**Men's Room near Physics Department, Princeton University**
Princeton, New Jersey

There was a young lady named Bright,
Whose speed was far faster than light;
She set out one day
In a relative way,
And returned home
the previous night.

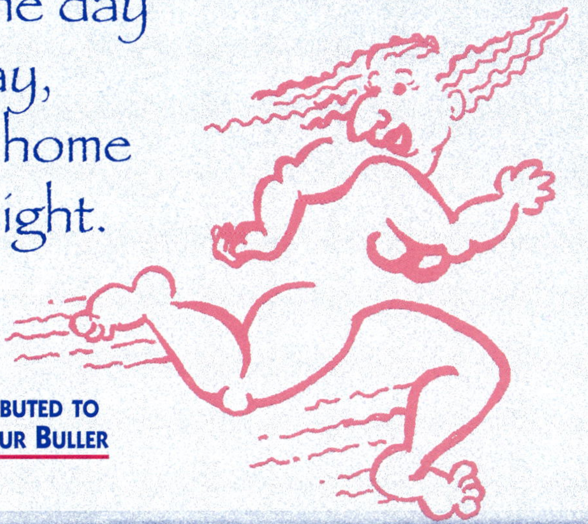

**ATTRIBUTED TO ARTHUR BULLER**

**MIT MEN'S ROOM**
CAMBRIDGE,
MASSACHUSETTS

No job is finished until the paperwork is done.

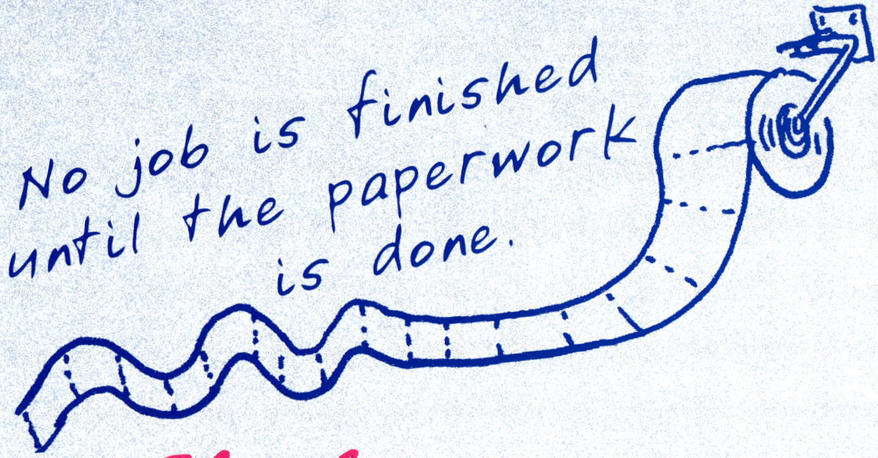

Flush twice — it's a long way to the lunchroom

**Stone Mountain High School**
Stone Mountain, Georgia

Pythagoras was a square

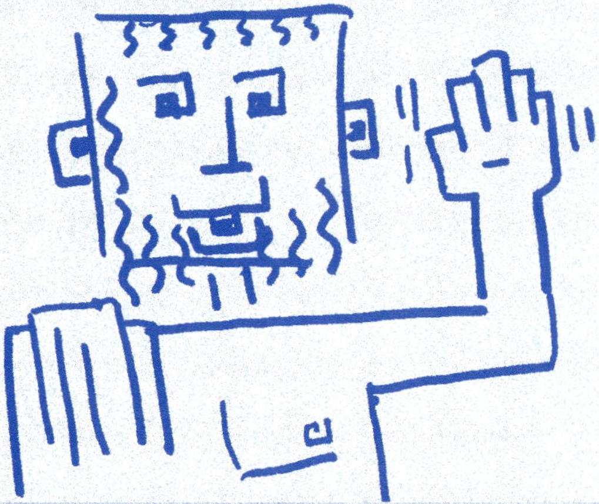

**Math Hall, PS 109**
New York, New York

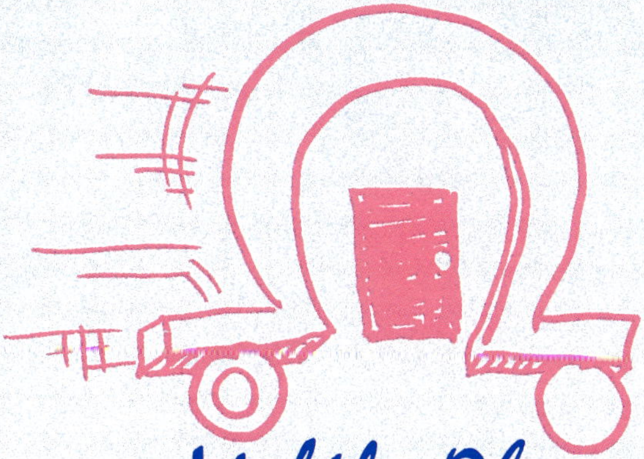

Mobile Ohm

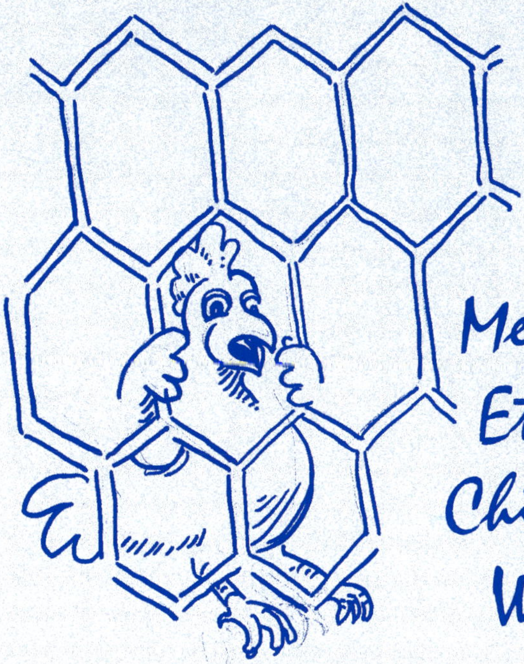

Methyl Ethyl Chicken Wire

Unless you're the LEAD DOG, the view never changes ...

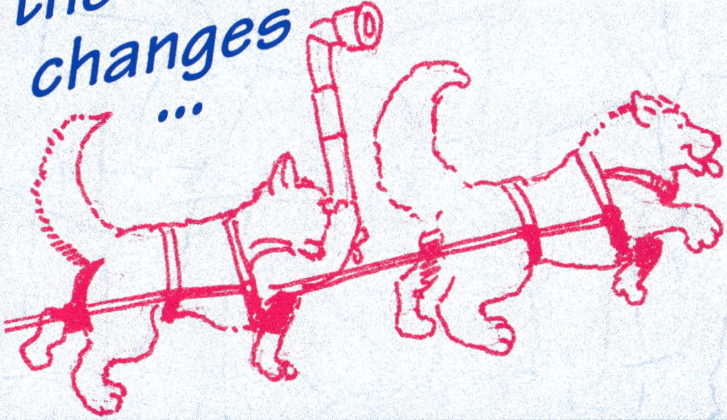

I used up all my sick days, so I'm calling in DEAD.

# getting ahead

U.S. POST OFFICE
BROOKLYN, NEW YORK

# ON THE JOB TRAINING ...

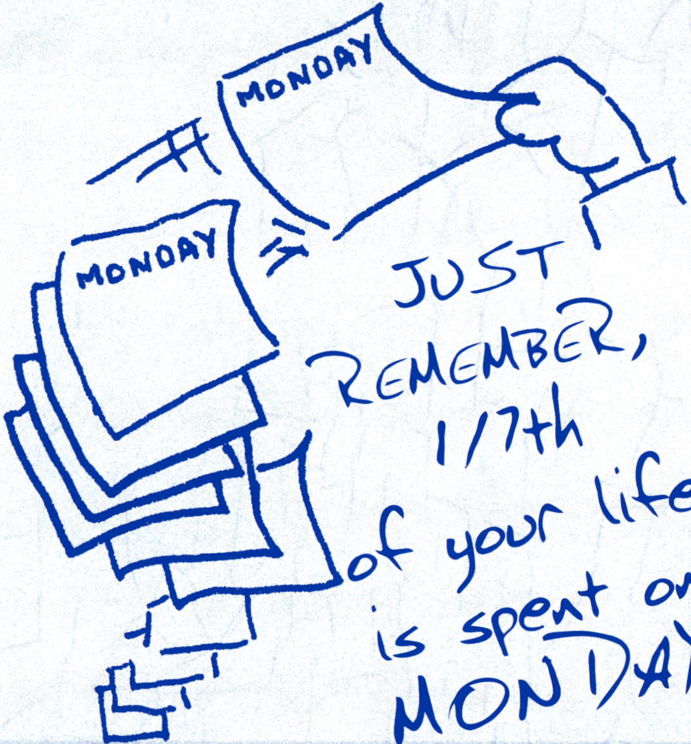


JUST REMEMBER, 1/7th of your life is spent on MONDAY!

BUDGET: a systematic way of going broke.

**CONGRESSIONAL BUDGET OFFICE, U.S. CAPITOL**
WASHINGTON, D.C.

THE BEATINGS WILL CONTINUE UNTIL MORALE IMPROVES!

**GM PLANT**
FLINT, MICHIGAN

DEPARTMENT OF REDUNDANCY DEPARTMENT

Around here, B.S. beats BRAINS.

It's not hard to meet expenses... they're EVERYWHERE!

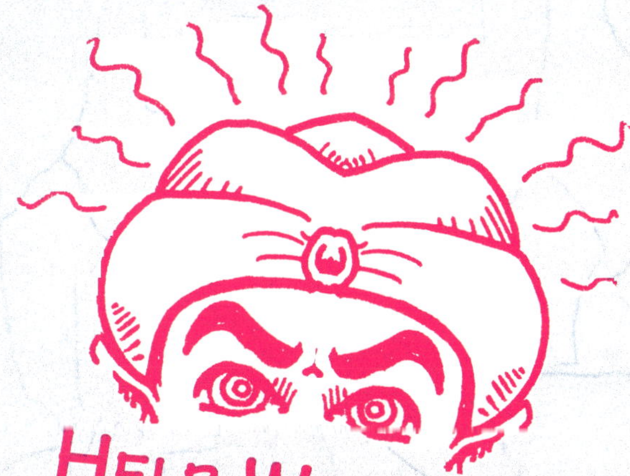

HELP WANTED: TELEPATH

(You know where to apply!)

**CHRYSLER BUILDING**
NEW YORK, NEW YORK

**CIA HEADQUARTERS**
LANGLEY, VIRGINIA

If I want your opinion, I'll ask you to fill out the necessary FORMS.

**Internal Revenue Service Center**
Philadelphia, Pennsylvania

I don't have a solution, but I admire the problem.

If things get any worse, I'll have to ask you to stop helping me.

**CETA Office Bathroom**
Los Angeles, California

I want to go
quietly in my sleep
like Grandpa...
not SCREAMING
IN TERROR
like his
passengers.

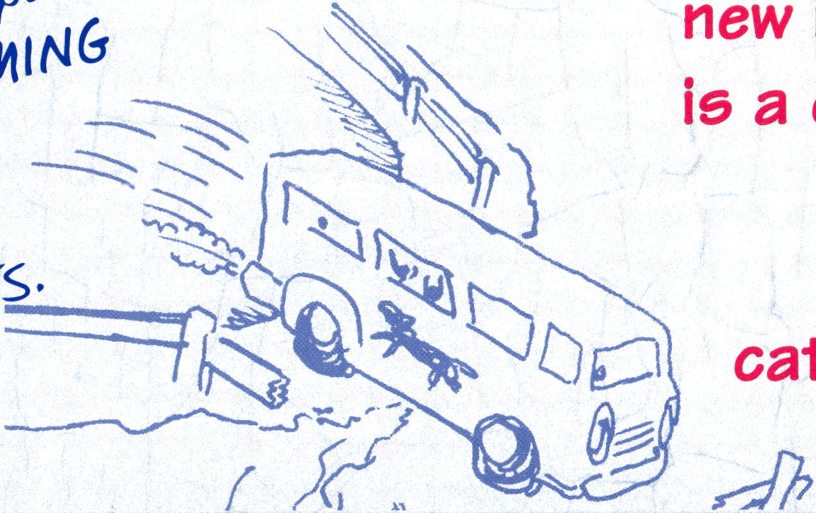

A man
with a
new idea
is a crank...

until it
catches on.

**GREYHOUND BUS STATION**
TERRE HAUTE, INDIANA

**WITH THANKS TO**
**MARK TWAIN**

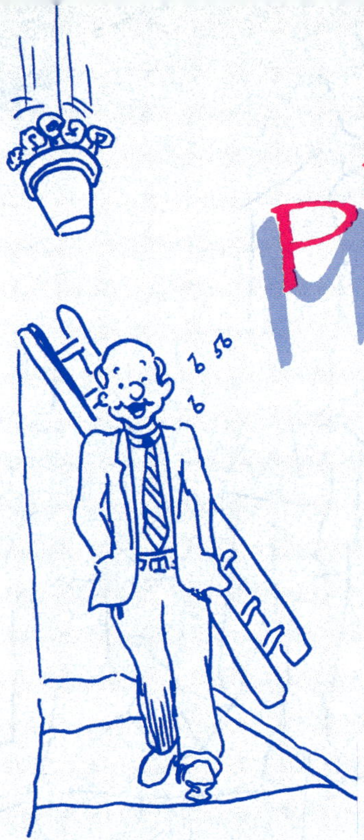

# Pharqel's Laws:

If anything CAN go wrong, it WILL.

If everything seems to be going well, you've overlooked SOMETHING!

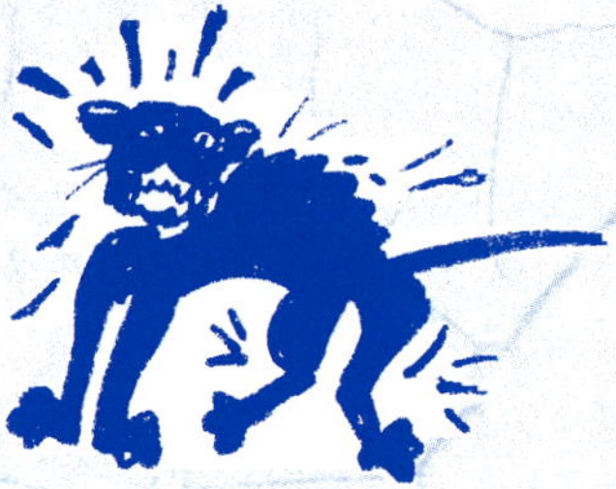

**DR. RICHARD'S VASECTOMY CLINIC**
PADUCAH, KENTUCKY

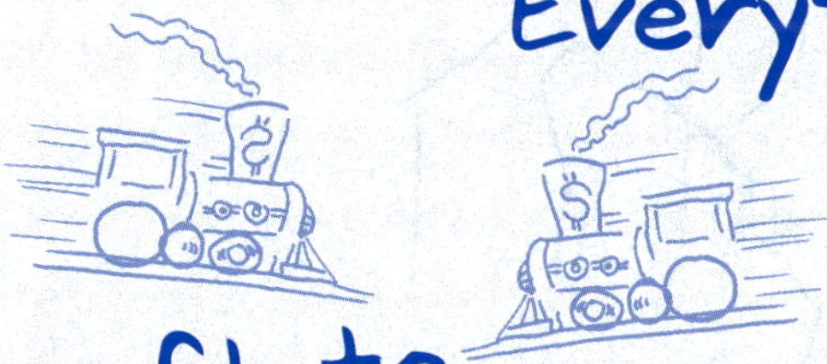

Everything **ALWAYS** costs more than budgeted.

Left to themselves, things will always go from **BAD** to **WORSE**.

When all else fails, read the **instructions**.

If at first you don't succeed... don't act **SURPRISED**.

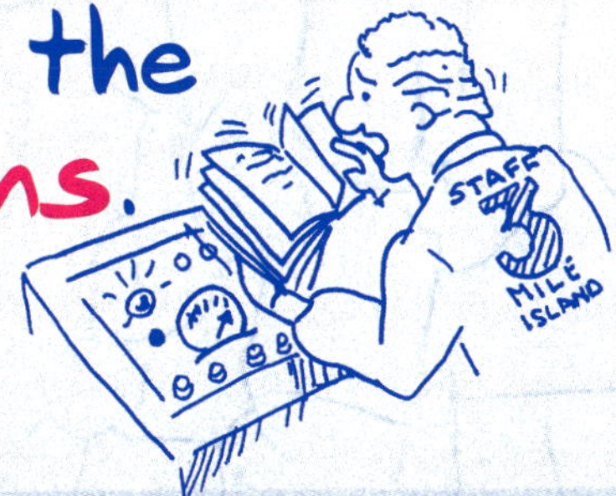


**UNITED STATES PAVILION**
**1982 WORLD'S FAIR**
KNOXVILLE, TENNESSEE

**NUCLEAR REACTOR**
**CONTAINMENT BUILDING**
THREE MILE ISLAND,
PENNSYLVANIA

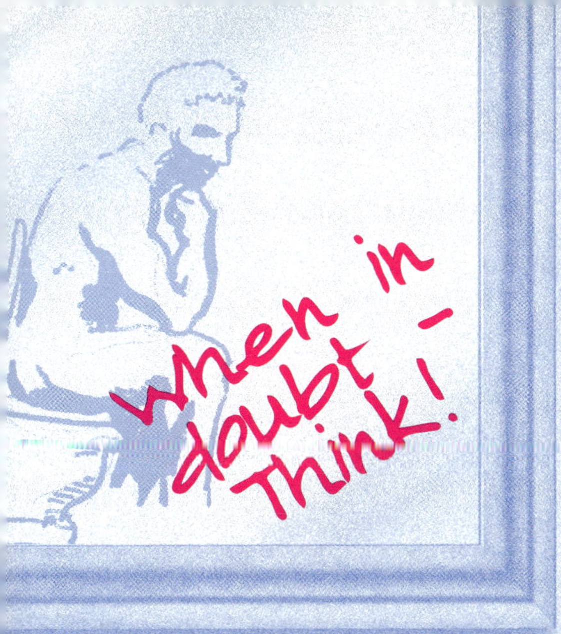

when in doubt – Think!

Don't put Descartes before Deshorses.

# reflections of a warped MIND

I think, therefore I am.
—Descartes

– I drink, therefore I am.

– I'm pink, therefore I'm Spam.

– I stink, therefore you smell.

## PHILOSOPHICALLY SPEAKING . . .

To do
is
to be
-Socrates

To be
is to do
- Sartre

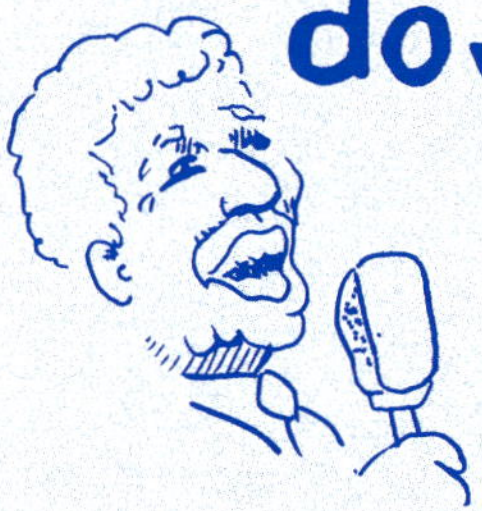

do be do be do be
doo!
-Sinatra

THE ONLY CURE FOR
STUPIDITY IS EVOLUTION.

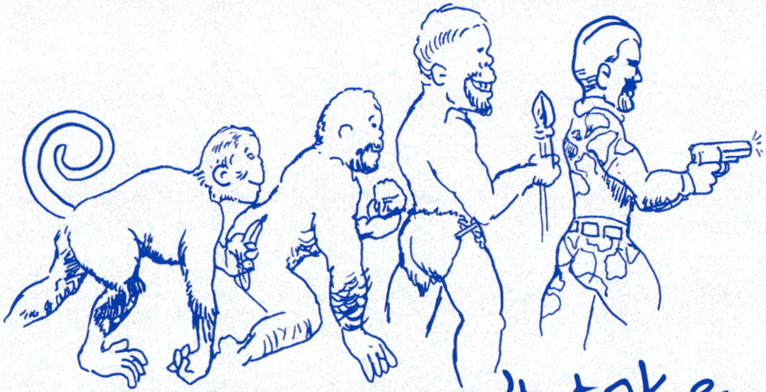

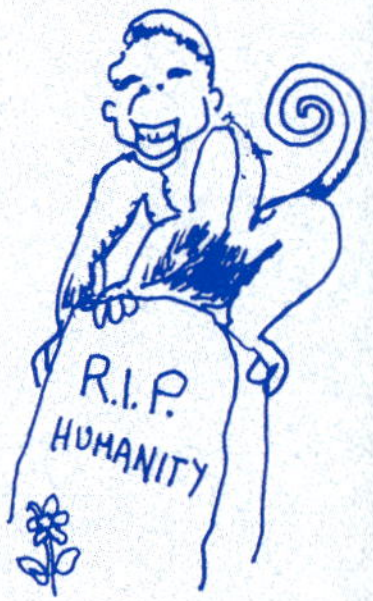


Evolution doesn't take
prisoners.

**3D FLOOR LAVATORY**
**NEW YORK MUSEUM**
**OF NATURAL HISTORY**
NEW YORK, NEW YORK

**SAN DIEGO ZOO**
SAN DIEGO, CALIFORNIA

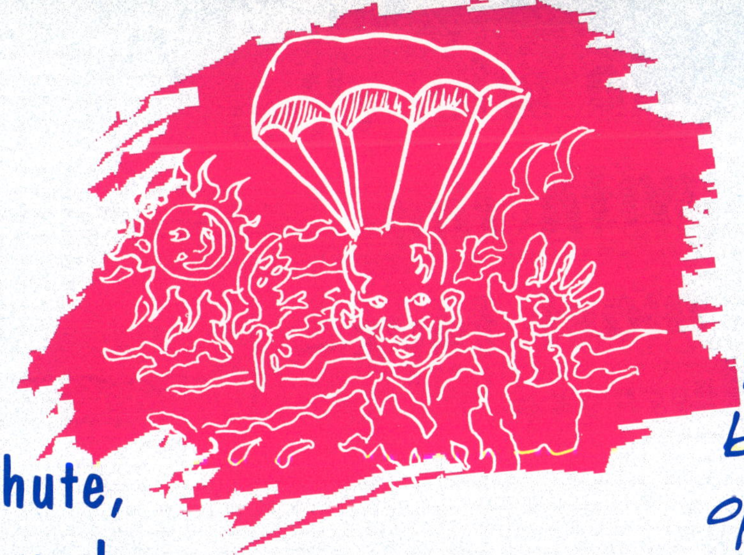

A mind
is like
a parachute,
it only works
when it's open...
and you're real high.

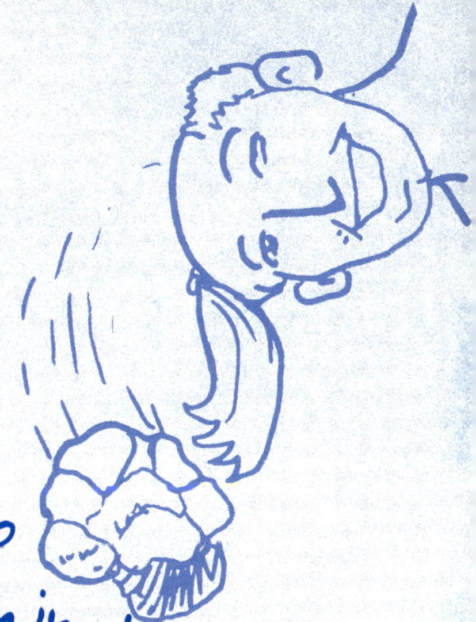

Don't
be too
open-minded...
your brains
might fall out.

MORAL MAJORITY
HEADQUARTERS
LYNCHBURG, VIRGINIA

Man's ambition
must be small
to write his name
on a bathroom wall.

Life's
a bitch,
then
you die.

He who dies
with the
most toys—
WINS.

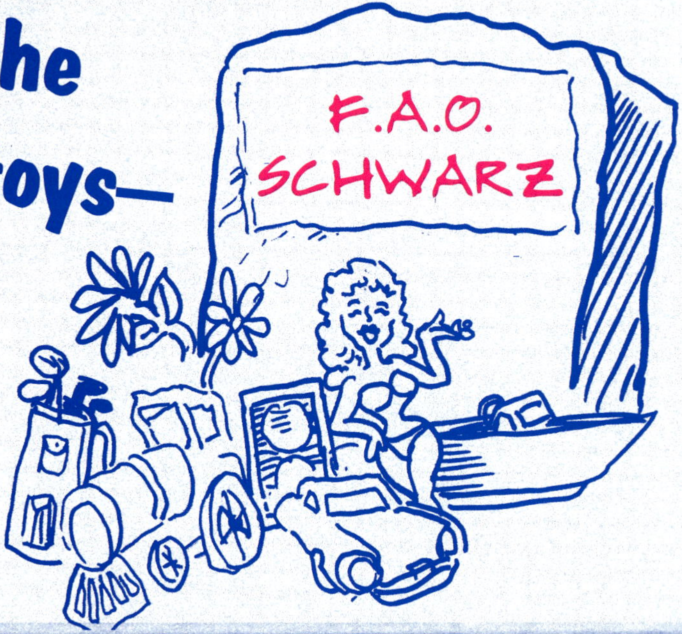


**BETTY FORD CLINIC**
**OUTPATIENT REST ROOM**
RANCHO MIRAGE, CALIFORNIA

# Get A Life!

– Can I buy one?

– Sure, I bought mine with a REALITY CHECK.

Take mine it's half-off!

– I'll get a life when someone proves it's better than what I already got.

**MEN'S ROOM, STUDIO 54**

NEW YORK, NEW YORK

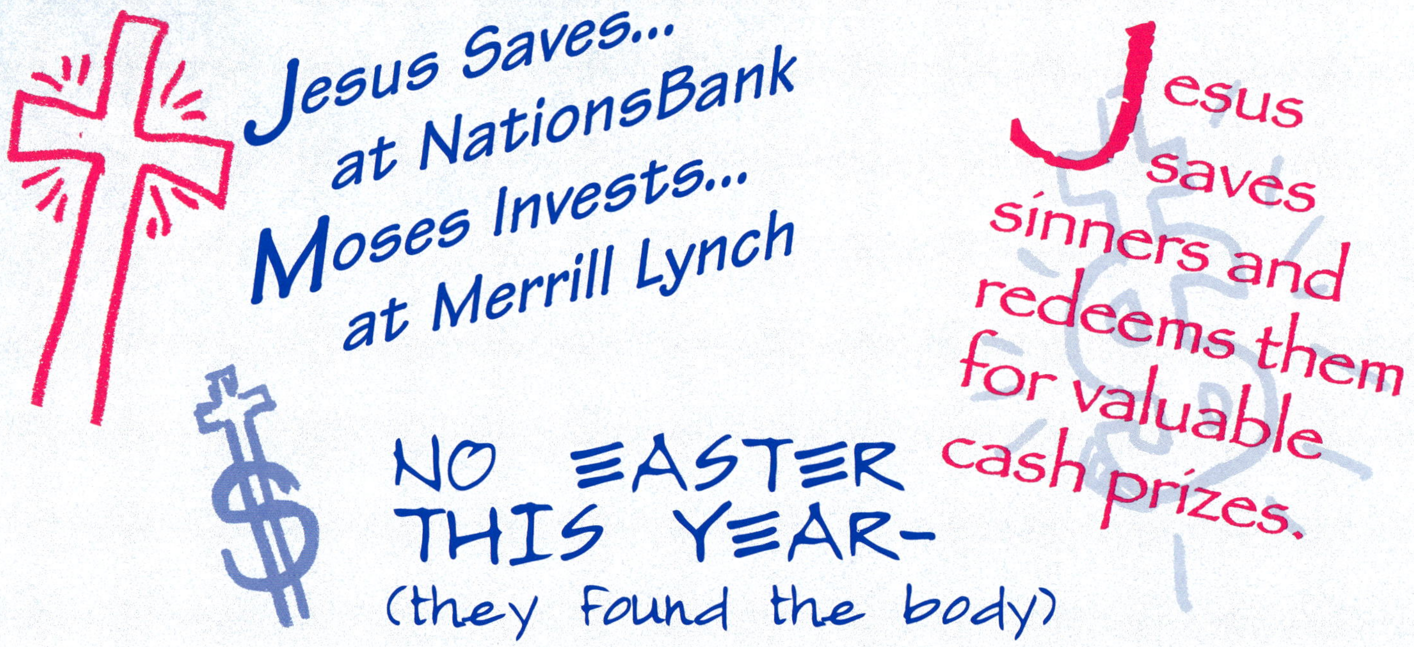


**Found Numerous Times Around the Country with the Names of Local Financial Institutions Substituted**

**Esso Station**
Bethlehem, Pennsylvania

We can't have a crisis TODAY—my schedule is already FULL.

If you've never been brainwashed, does that mean you have a dirty mind?

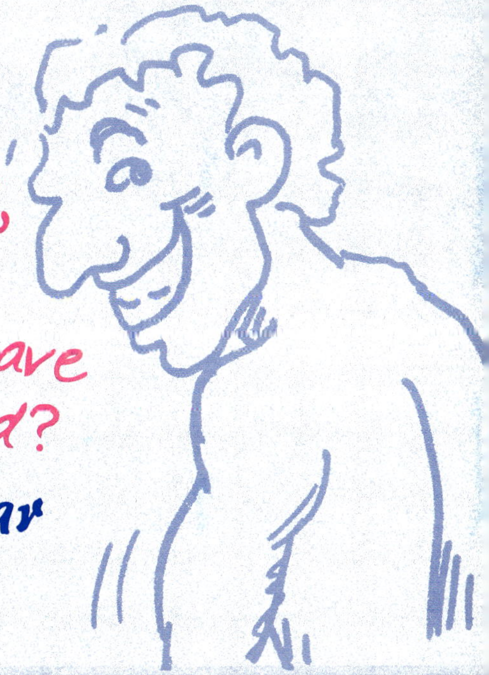

**Believe nothing of what you hear and only half of what you see.**

American Society of Psychic Research
Enigma, Georgia

Pizza Hut
Waco, Texas

Just because you're PARANOID doesn't mean they are NOT out to get you.

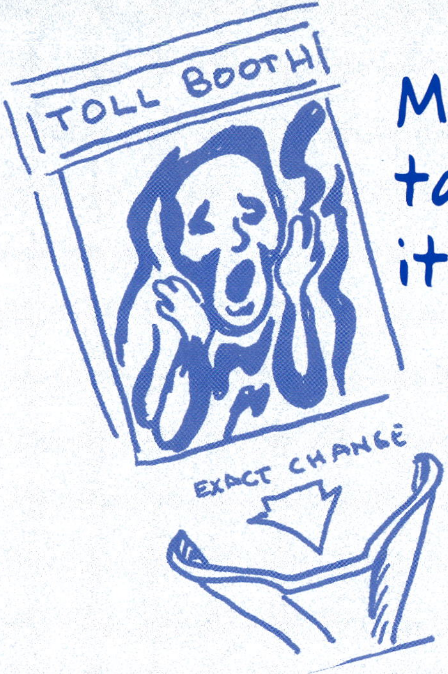


Madness takes its toll... please have exact change.

DON'T LOOK BACK... they might be gaining on you!

**HOUSE UNAMERICAN ACTIVITIES COMMITTEE HEARING ROOM**
WASHINGTON, D.C.

Roses are Red—
Violets are
Blue—
I'm schizophrenic.
—and so
am I!

REALITY
is what
refuses
to go away
when I stop
believing
in it.

**A conclusion is simply the point at which you got tired of thinking.**

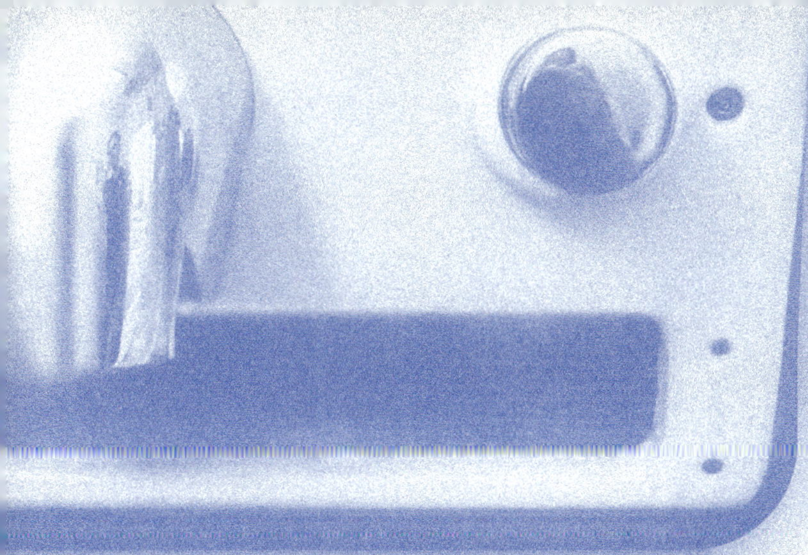

# MORE hot air

Bore: A person who talks when you wish him to listen.

AMBROSE BIERCE

To hear speech by Nixon, press button.

~~Bush~~ ~~Carter~~

~~Reagan~~ Clinton

# WASHING OUR HANDS OF POLITICIANS . . .

Reagan could screw up a one-man parade in a ghost town.

I've given up anarchy. Too many rules.

THE FARM COMMUNE
TENNESSEE

What's Long and Hangs in Front of An Asshole?

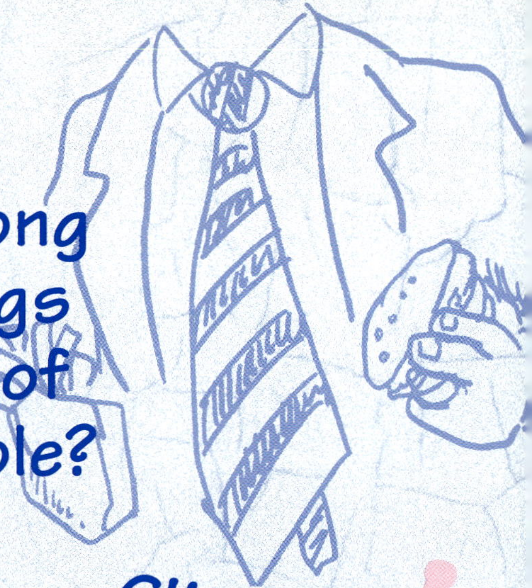

Clinton's Tie

AMERICAN OPINION BOOKSTORE
OMAHA, NEBRASKA

# DIPLOMACY...

...the art of letting someone have your way

...the art of saying "nice doggie" until you can get your hands on a big stick.

**UNITED NATIONS BUILDING**
NEW YORK, NEW YORK

The pen is mightier than the sword, but the Keyboard is mightier than the ICBM

**CATO INSTITUTE**
WASHINGTON, D.C.

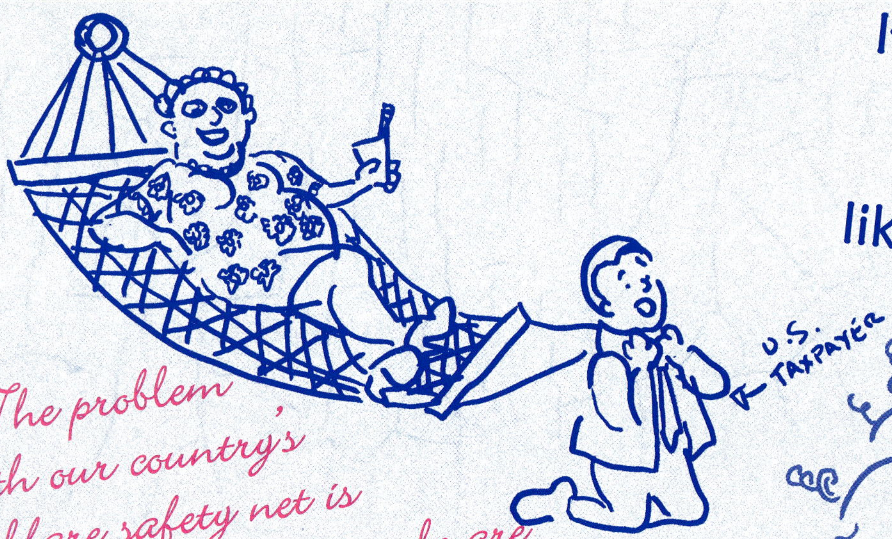


*The problem with our country's welfare safety net is that too many people are using it as a hammock.*

**If you stand between the hogs and the trough, you're very likely to get trampled.**

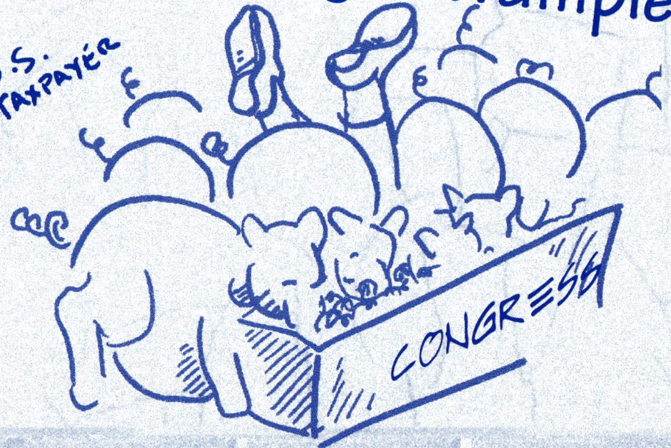


**Social Security Office**
Tampa, Florida

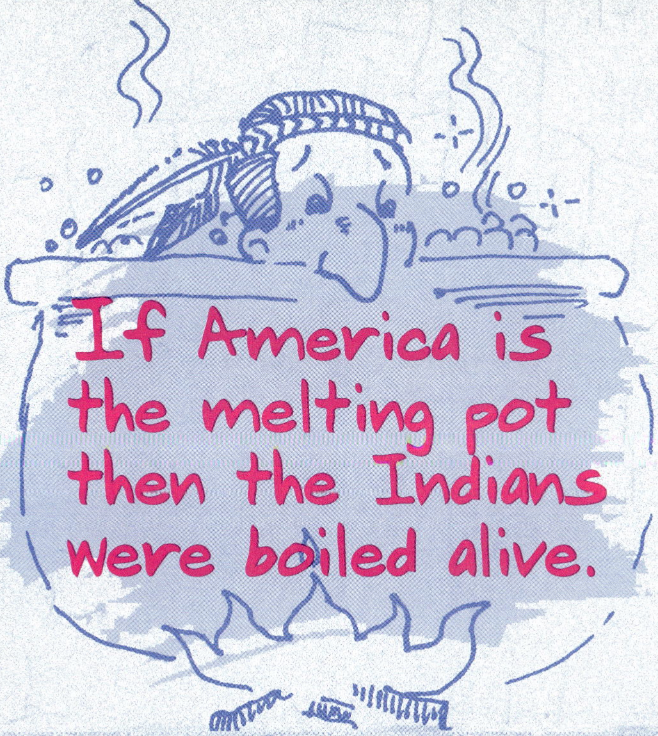


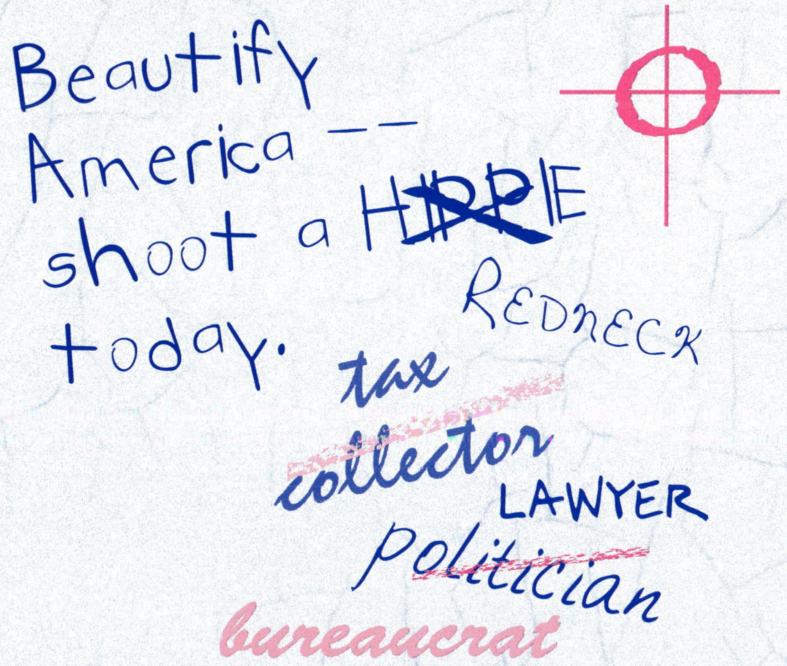


**SEQUOIA SOUVENIR STORE**
CHEROKEE, NORTH CAROLINA

# DEMOCRACY...

...three WOLVES and a SHEEP voting on what to have for LUNCH.

BACK OF BUS SEAT
SELMA, ALABAMA

...the worship of JACKALS by JACKASSES.

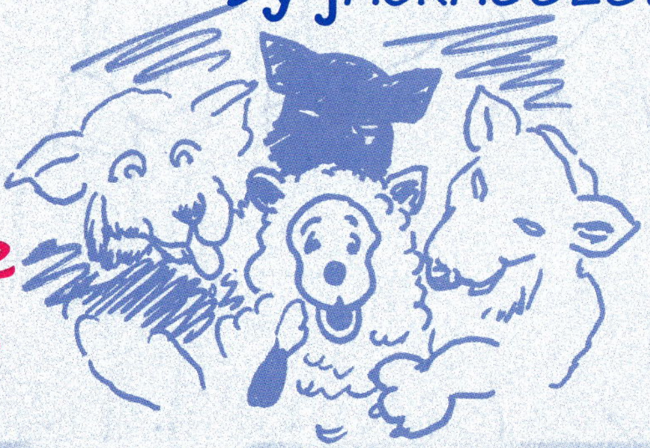

THANKS TO
H.L. MENCKEN

I'm not a member of any organized political party—I'm a Democrat.

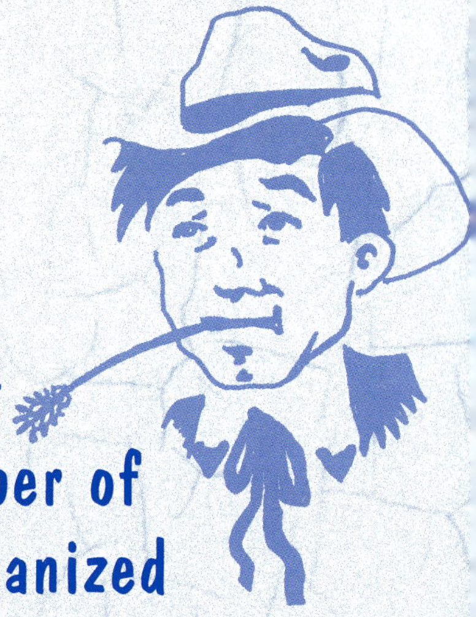

ATTRIBUTED
TO WILL ROGERS

VOTE EARLY
AND
VOTE OFTEN.

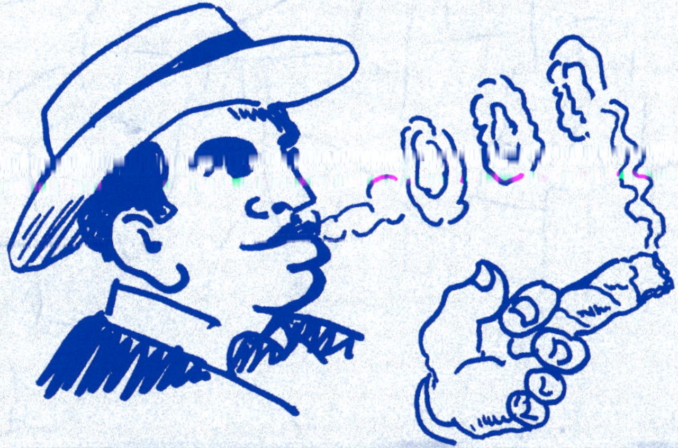

Old Chicago
Proverb Attributed
To Al Capone

I don't fear fascism...
our government isn't
that ORGANIZED!

ACLU
Washington, D.C.

No one will ever
go BROKE
underestimating
the taste of the
American public.

Thanks to
H.L. Mencken
... again

When you hear someone talking about the need to make sacrifices...

start looking for the ALTAR they're going to drag you to!

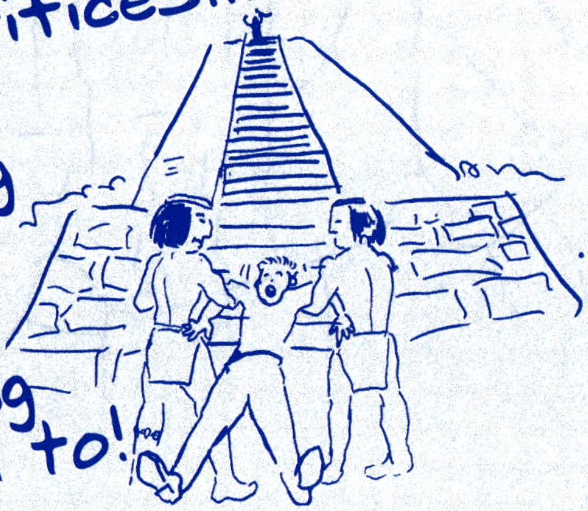

GOVERNMENT PROVIDED HEALTHCARE: the COMPASSION of the IRS... ...the EFFICIENCY of the POST OFFICE... and the THRIFT of the PENTAGON.

**White House Press Room**
Washington, D.C.

**Executive Washroom, Rose Law Firm**
Little Rock, Arkansas

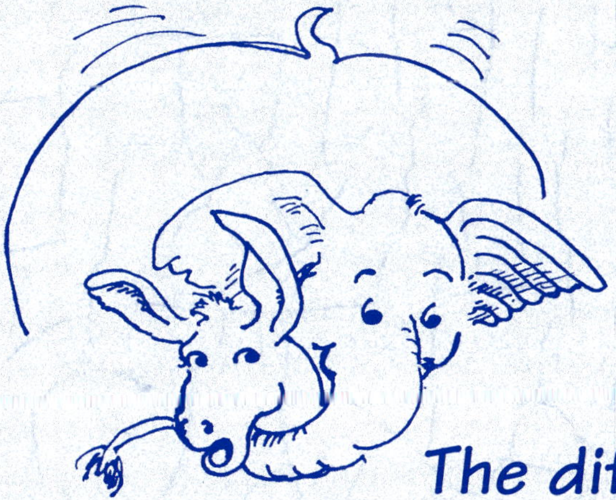

The difference between Democrats and Republicans is like the difference between SYPHILIS and GONORRHEA.

**Libertarian Party Headquarters**
Washington, D.C.

Socialist: A person who has yearnings for someone else's earnings.

**Wharton School of Business**
Philadelphia, Pennsylvania

# words of WISDOM

God gave us memories that we might have roses in December.

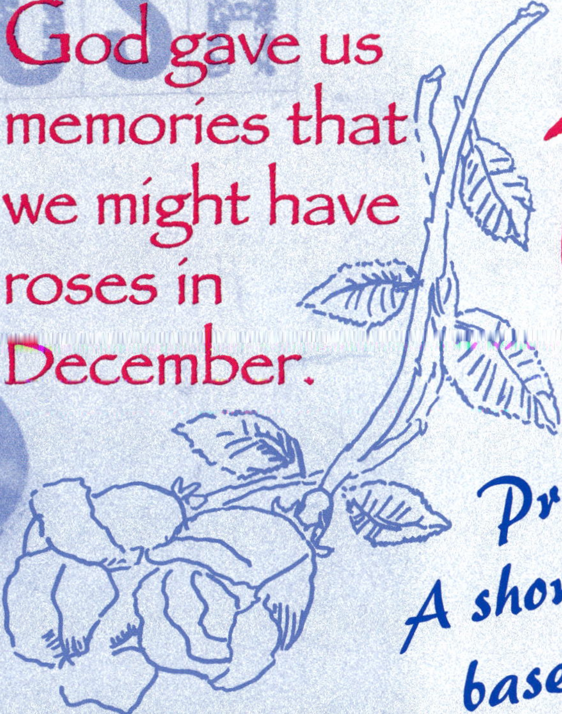

*Proverb:*
*A short sentence based on long experience.*

## Follow At Your Own Risk . . .

# NEVER...

...wrestle with a pig. You just get dirty and the pig enjoys it.

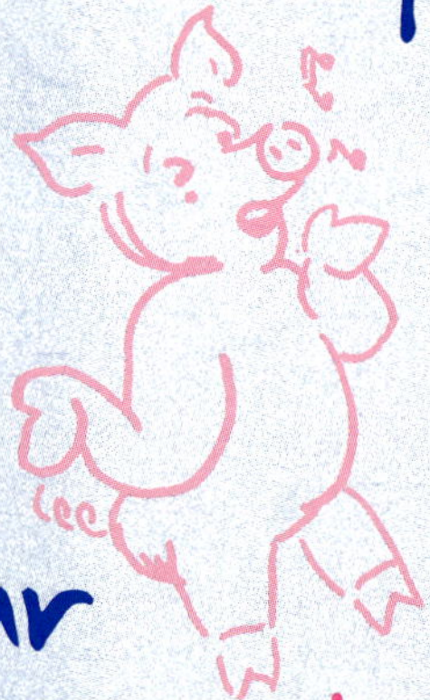

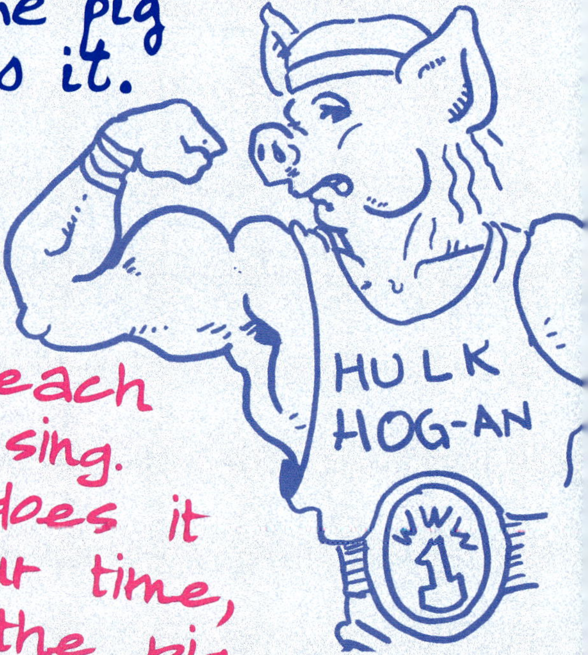


...risk your money on a poor man's advice.

**NEW YORK STOCK EXCHANGE**
WALL STREET,
NEW YORK

...try to teach a pig to sing. Not only does it waste your time, it annoys the pig.

Chaste is she whom none have asked.

**St. Mary's Convent**
Salt Lake City, Utah

*A lady is a woman who can make a man act like a gentleman.*

**The Mustang Ranch**
Nevada

Be nice to your children; they get to pick your nursing home.

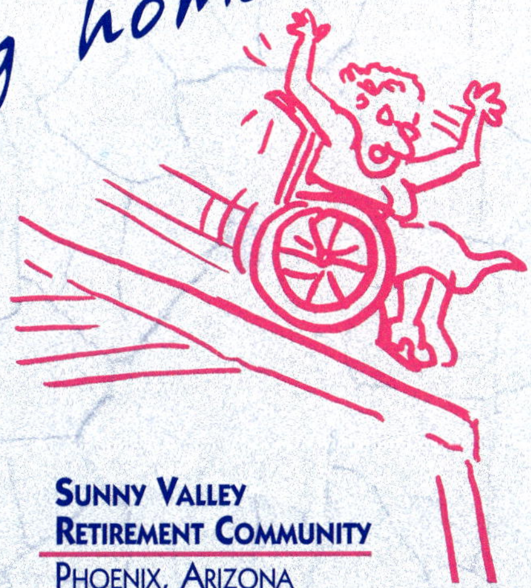

**Sunny Valley Retirement Community**
Phoenix, Arizona

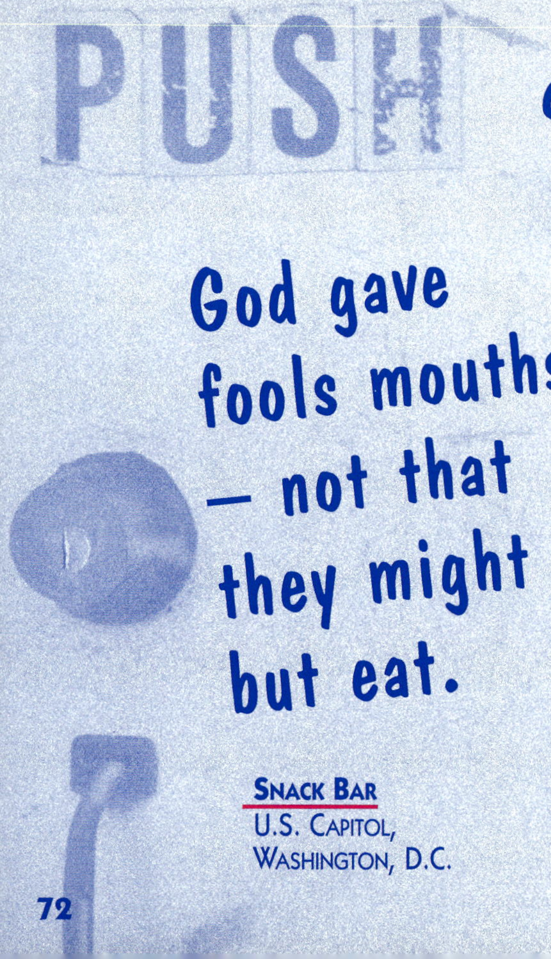


ONE GOOD PAIR OF EARS CAN DRY A THOUSAND TONGUES.

God gave fools mouths — not that they might talk, but eat.

**SNACK BAR**
U.S. CAPITOL,
WASHINGTON, D.C.

One's nose is never so happy as when thrust into the affairs of another.

**AMBROSE BIERCE**

He who sues over a sheep loses his cow.

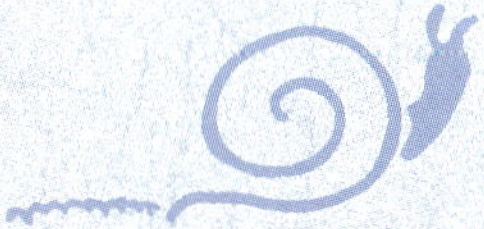

By perseverance the snail reached the ark.

**L'ESCARGOT FRENCH RESTAURANT**
SAN FRANCISCO, CALIFORNIA

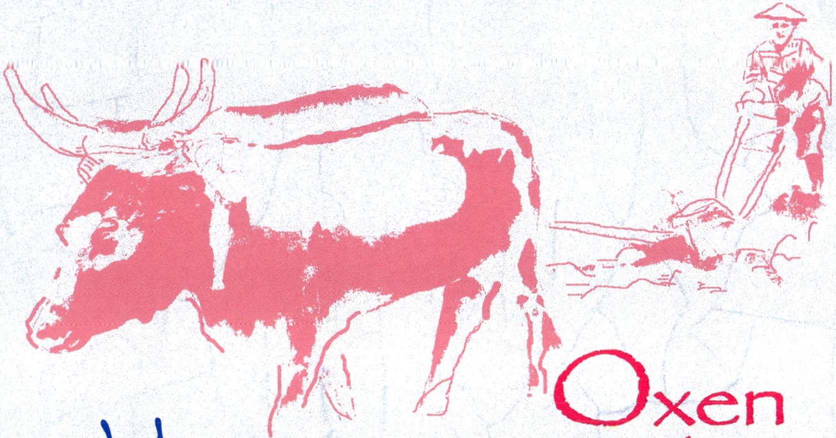

Old foxes need no tutors.

**OFFICES OF THE LEAGUE OF WOMEN VOTERS**
HOUSTON, TEXAS

Oxen are slow, but the earth is patient.

**RED DRAGON CHINESE RESTAURANT**
CHINATOWN, NEW YORK, NEW YORK

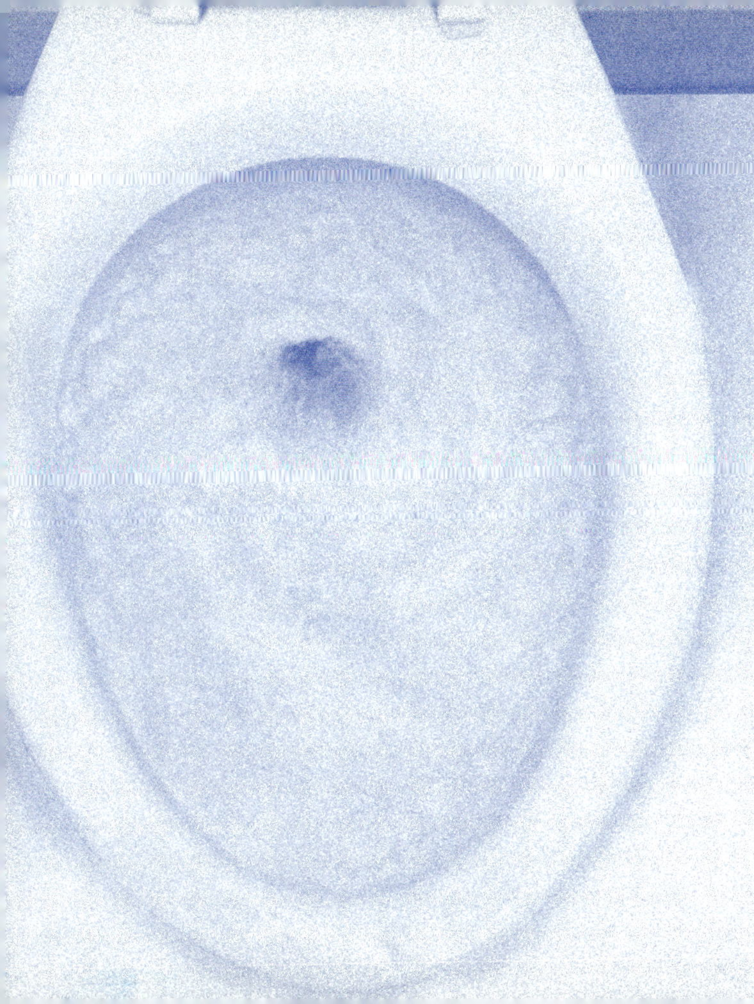

# scatological thinking

**WARNING:**
THE FOLLOWING PAGES CONTAIN MATERIAL THAT MAY NOT BE SUITABLE FOR ALL AGE GROUPS.

PARENTS, GET YOUR KIDS TO EXPLAIN.

## THESE WE SHOULD HAVE FLUSHED . . .

If, you shake it more than twice -
you're playing with it!

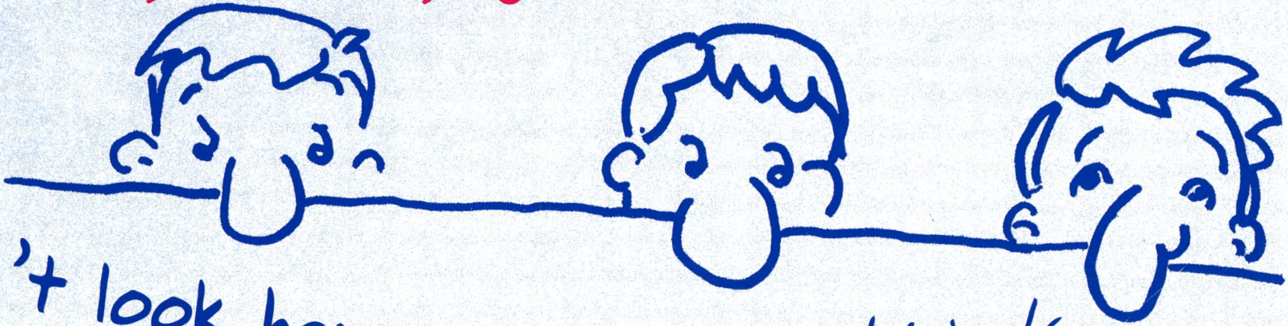

Don't look here.
The joke is in
your hand!

**CATCH A RISING STAR**
NEW YORK, NEW YORK

You may think
you're American,
but European.

**ELLIS ISLAND**
NEW YORK, NEW YORK

We aim to please... you aim too, please.

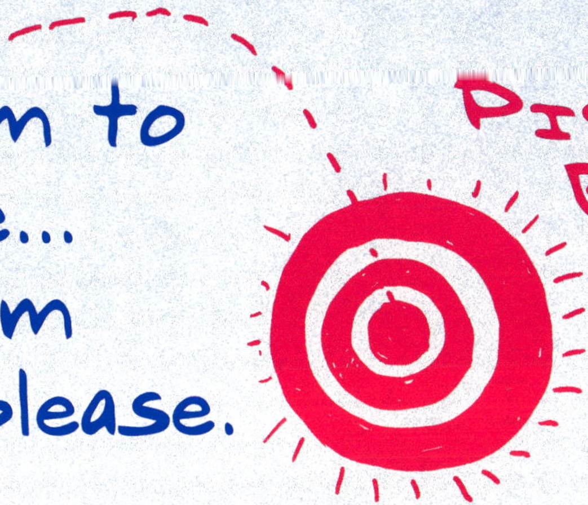

ANYONE CAN PISS ON THE FLOOR. BE MY HERO — CRAP ON THE CEILING.

Look out for #1. Don't step in #2.

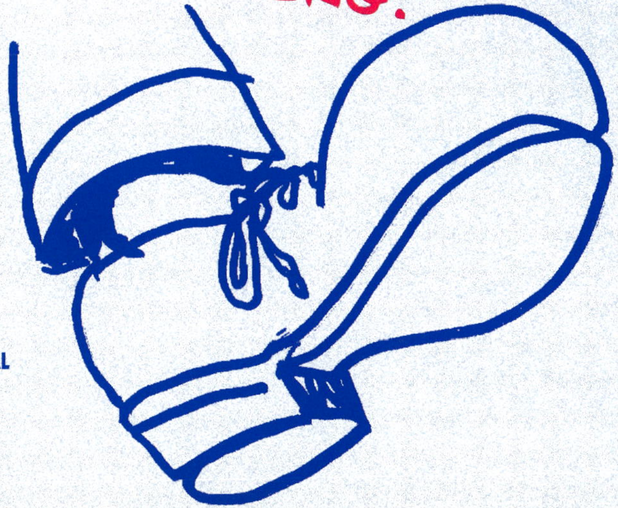

**HERTZ CAR RENTAL**
**O'HARE AIRPORT**
CHICAGO, ILLINOIS

JULY 17, 1986:
VOYAGER FINDS RINGS
AROUND URANUS

Sounds like a case for
Preparation H

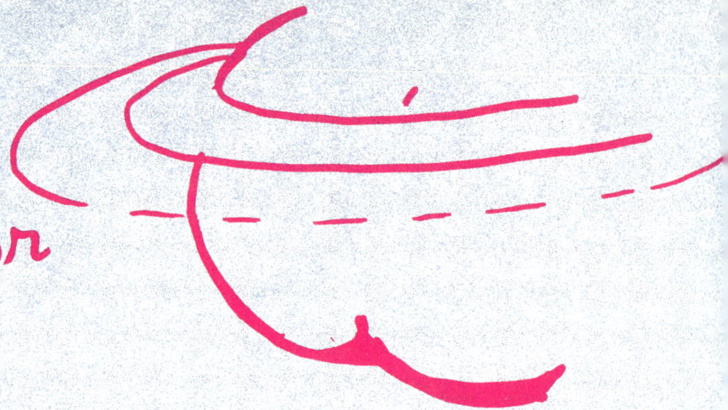

Farts smell
so that deaf
people can
enjoy them
too!

**STUDENT CENTER, GALLAUDET UNIVERSITY**
WASHINGTON, D.C.

**MARSHALL SPACE FLIGHT CENTER**
HUNTSVILLE, ALABAMA

Here I sit
all brokenhearted...
came to crap
and only farted.

IN THE DAYS OF PAY TOILETS:
"HERE I SIT ALL BROKENHEARTED
PAID MY DIME AND ONLY FARTED."

**GREYHOUND BUS STATION**
WINSTON-SALEM, NORTH CAROLINA

START A
MOVEMENT –
EAT A PRUNE.

**UNIVERSITY OF CALIFORNIA**
BERKELEY, CALIFORNIA

Don't bother to squat -
Might as well have a seat
Cause the crabs around here
can jump 50 feet.

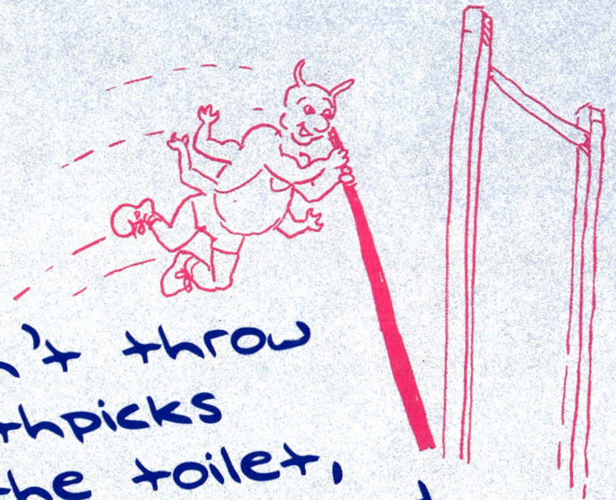

THEY TOOK MY PENCIL
THEY TOOK MY PEN,
BUT THE CRAP HOUSE
POET HAS STRUCK AGAIN.

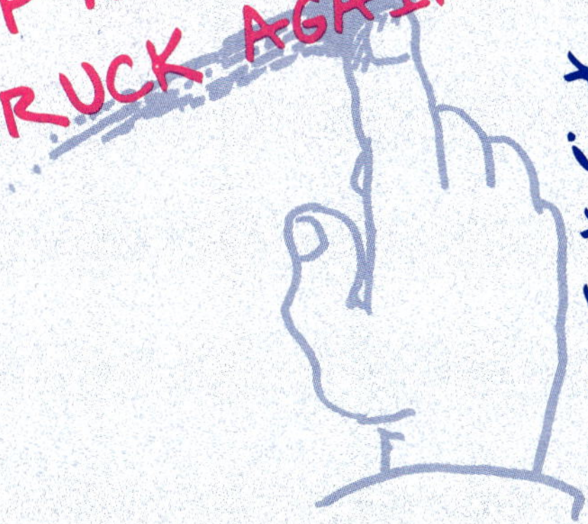

Don't throw
toothpicks
in the toilet,
the crabs around
here can
pole vault.

**OLYMPIC STADIUM**
ATLANTA, GEORGIA

On the long hard road only the hard last long.

**VICTORIA'S SECRET**
**LENOX SQUARE**
ATLANTA, GEORGIA

A GOOD man is HARD to find.

A HARD man is GOOD to find.

**STUDENT CENTER**
**RADCLIFFE COLLEGE**
CAMBRIDGE, MASSACHUSETTS

He offered her honor
She honored his offer
and all the night long
it was on her and off her.

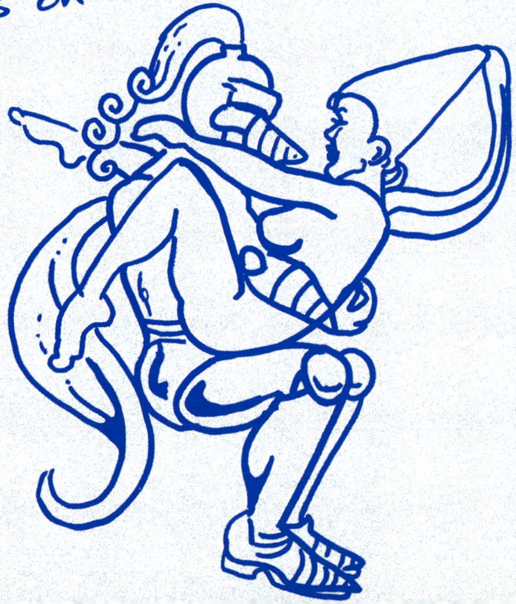

All I ask
is some
peace and
quiet –
give me a
piece and
I'll be quiet.

**GRACELAND WEDDING CHAPEL**
LAS VEGAS, NEVADA

This guy I knew
from the lodge
Had straps installed
in his Dodge
Once his girl
was strapped in
He committed a sin
Without even leaving
the garage.

My car
may not be
the Mayflower,
but your daughter
came across
in it!

I strangled
Linda Lovelace!

Kinky is
using a feather;
Perverted is
using the whole
chicken.

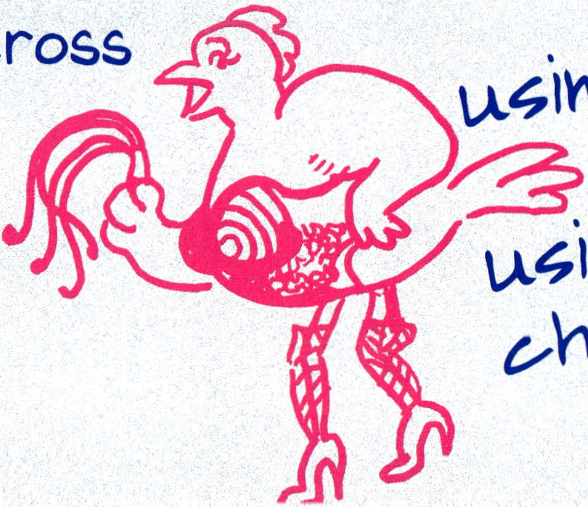

**PLATO'S RETREAT**
NEW YORK,
NEW YORK

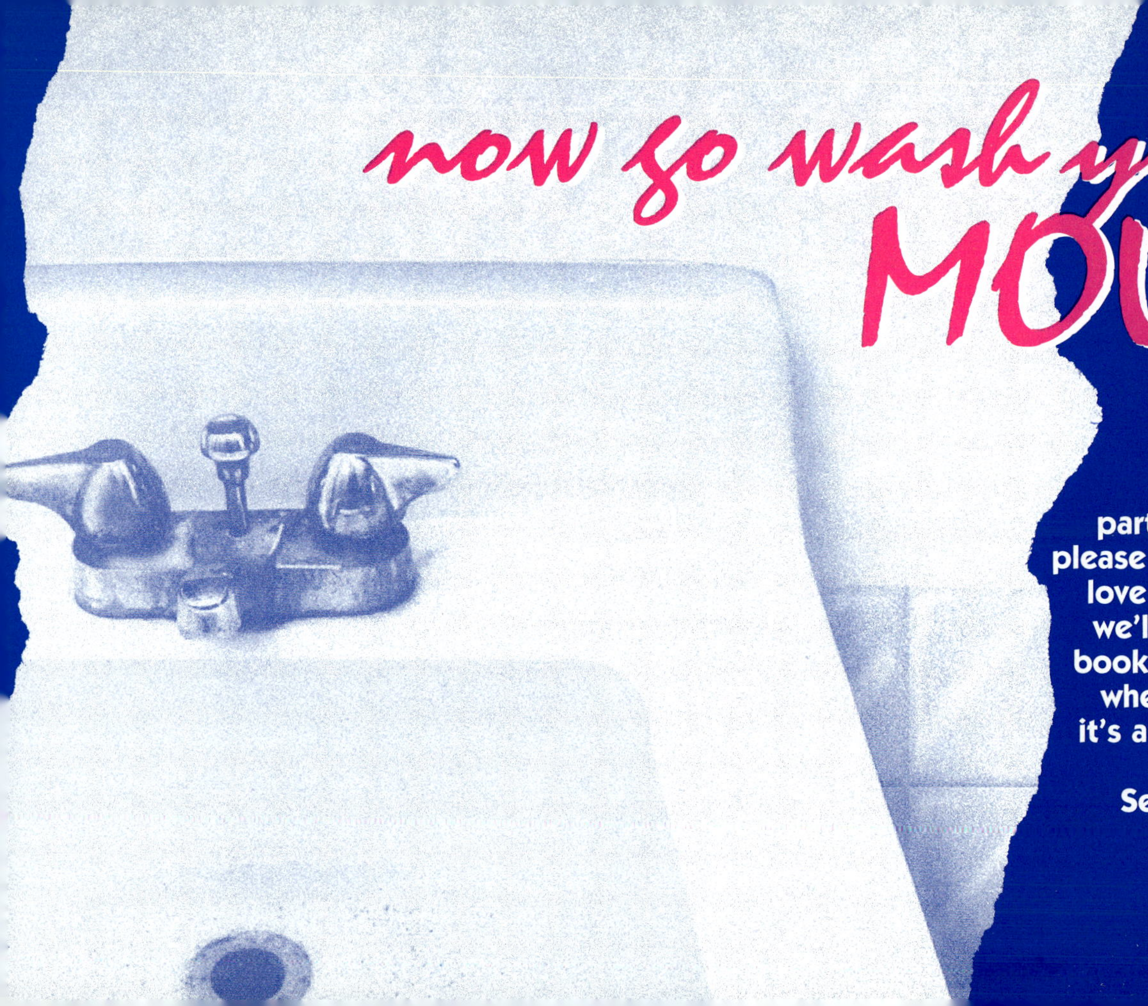

# *now go wash your* MOUTH *out*

If you've seen some particularly clever graffiti, please share it with us– we'd love to see it. If we like it, we'll include it in our next book. Write it down, tell us where you found it and if it's a drawing– photograph it and send us a copy. Send all your graffiti to:

Off the Wall
c/o The Graffiti Guys
P.O. Box 13402
Atlanta, GA 30324